THE RELATE GUIDE
TO SECOND FAMILIES

THE
RELATE GUIDE
TO SECOND FAMILIES

*Living successfully with other
people's children*

Suzie Hayman

VERMILION
London

1 3 5 7 9 10 8 6 4 2

First published in the United Kingdom in 1997 by Vermilion
an imprint of Ebury Press
Random House
20 Vauxhall Bridge Road
London SW1V 2SA

Random House Australia (Pty) Limited
18 Poland Road, Glenfield
Auckland 10, New Zealand

Random House South Africa (Pty) Limited
Endulini, 5A Jubilee Road
Parktown 2193, South Africa

Random House UK Limited Reg. No. 954009

A catalogue record for this book is available from the British Library

ISBN: 0 09 181358 1

Printed and bound in Great Britain by Mackays of Chatham, plc

This book is dedicated to the
memory of Jan Laithwaite

CONTENTS

Acknowledgements

Many thanks to Suzy Powling, Derek Hill, Julia Cole and Marj Thoburn at Relate and all the families who allowed me to use their stories. I am especially grateful to Norma Heaton, who was supervisor at Kendal Relate during my counselling training and gave me so much.

Thanks also to Sarah Sutton at Ebury for her encouragement and patience.

FOREWORD

Second families are first and foremost the expression of the adult partners' love for one another and their desire to create a 'safe haven' for their children and for themselves. They offer us strong evidence that 'family values' are alive and well in our society. The many stories of the happiness and security they have brought to men, women and children have prompted RELATE to add this book about them to its series dealing with human relationships.

Perhaps the most striking thing about second families is how much more varied they are than first families. They challenge many of our assumptions about what is necessary if people are to live happy and fulfilling lives together. They teach object lessons about the ways in which differences can be a source of rich experiences within families. Their networks of relationships and their sometimes complicated domestic arrangements reveal how resourceful people can be when they are committed to building families and creating environments in which young and old can flourish.

That is not to deny that second families may face intractable problems and can fail. There are many stories about such situations and a body of folklore which, if accepted uncritically, can be the source of great discouragement. One of the purposes of this book is to try to strike a realistic balance when exploring the nature of those families and to identify the issues and the influences that trouble them and fuel the myths.

The complicated nature of some second families, which cartoonists and comedians latch on to, can obscure the fact that basically we all have the same needs for love, security and success, and the same fears about others' disapproval, and of isolation and failure. It is in going back to those basics that this book offers ways of thinking about second families that immediately make them more understandable. It is our hope that that understanding will help readers to find their own ways to fulfil their hopes for a family life that meets the needs of all its members.

Derek Hill
Relate Head of Counselling

Grant me the courage to change the things I can change, the serenity to accept the things I cannot change and the wisdom to know the difference.

Reinhold Nieburh

PART ONE
SECOND TIME AROUND

1

THE COUPLE RELATIONSHIP IN SECOND FAMILIES

I got married for the first time when I was 19. I had a white wedding with all the trimmings. I wore a long, white dress and a veil, and had four bridesmaids. It was in a church and all my family and loads of friends came, and we had this ginormous reception at a local hotel, with a band and a sit-down meal. It cost my dad thousands but he thought it was worth it and so did I. You see, I thought it was going to be the only wedding I ever had. I thought we were going to live happily ever after, no troubles in the world. Well, the second time I got married was in a registry office and I was 31. My mum was there and my sister but my dad and brother wouldn't come. But I was happy because although I'd seen my first marriage go down I thought I knew exactly why. I thought, this time I'll get it right. I was a lot more realistic about what to expect, like knowing that you don't stay madly in love all your life. But the one mistake I did make was thinking I was starting all over again with a clean sheet. I hadn't realised that a second marriage has problems of its own.

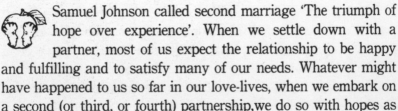 Samuel Johnson called second marriage 'The triumph of hope over experience'. When we settle down with a partner, most of us expect the relationship to be happy and fulfilling and to satisfy many of our needs. Whatever might have happened to us so far in our love-lives, when we embark on a second (or third, or fourth) partnership, we do so with hopes as

high, if not higher, than when we set up home the first time. We may have different expectations from a second relationship but many of us still hold the same belief that we will live 'happily ever after'. We may be right, but unfortunately our expectations often turn out to be unrealistic. One reason for this is that we tend to assume that good relationships come about naturally, without much effort on our part. There are pitfalls in any relationship, whatever the circumstances, but second relationships come with quite a few extra potential problem areas and knowing about them can be a great help. The aim of this book is to explore the problems and discuss why difficulties may arise in a second family. Once you understand why you and those around you feel and act the way you do, you can make changes, if you choose. You will find help with exploring and understanding second family relationships, as well as practical suggestions for ways in which you and everyone involved can actually do something to improve your situation.

This book is for anyone involved in a second (or third, or so-forth) family, where one or both of you have previously been involved in a significant relationship, married or unmarried. When someone has been in a relationship before, you can experience a range of problems that may vary in intensity. Either or both of you may suffer feelings of guilt, hurt, jealousy, envy, anger or fear of rejection. If children from one or both earlier relationships are brought to these new partnerships, it can heighten the problems. Two adults without children are just as much a family as any group that includes children, however, and the mixture of feelings may be present anyway – kids are simply a visible and indelible reminder that this is not a first-time match.

If there are children in your family, they are likely to need your understanding and help to come to terms with the changes they will experience as you establish and develop your second relationship. Their feelings and their reactions will obviously have an effect on how you and your partner manage your new partnership. But it is a mistake to think that on their own two adults will have no problems in a new relationship. Equally, children are not the only ones who might experience difficulties in adjusting to a second family, and focusing mainly on them will not solve all the problems that may arise. The fact is that the couple relationship is the main relationship in any family group, whether you have two or 10 children. If the couple have a relationship that is healthy and functioning, the family will also be healthy and functioning, or well on its way to being so. If any family member seems to be having a hard time, focusing on and 'fixing' the couple relationship is often the best way of setting it right.

You, or someone close to you, may feel the situation is fully under control and you do not need any adjustment. Or you may be in the throes of such extreme conflict that you are convinced nothing that anyone can say or do will ever make it better. Whichever end of the spectrum you are at, or at whatever point in between, you could find the information and suggestions in this book useful. It is worth noting, however, that the only person you can change is yourself. No amount of helping, hectoring or badgering other people is going to make them change if they don't want to. But changing your own behaviour and feelings will often cause such an alteration in the balance of your family, that everyone around will fall into new and often better patterns.

MAKING CHANGES

Any group of people who are in contact with each other will have arguments and disagreements from time to time, and families (with or without children) are no exception to this. When your family is a second one, you may find these arguments seem more bitter, longer and harder to resolve. You may feel that all your problems are the fault of an ex-partner, yourself for not trying harder, or an unruly child. In short, you may well feel that the people in this situation are to blame. If you are going to make your situation better, there are three steps you can take that will carry you towards a solution.

The first is to EXPLORE – to look at what is happening in yourself and in those around you.

The second is to UNDERSTAND – to see why you feel and act the way you do and what you might do about it.

The third is to ACT – to make changes in your responses and behaviour to bring about the arrangement you would like.

Exploration, understanding and action are the three stages of change that counsellors use to help an individual, couple or family transform a problem into a solution. None of them work in isolation. Talking about a situation hardly helps on its own. Achieving understanding isn't like being given a magic wand. Just because you know *why* you feel and act the way you do, doesn't mean that everything will automatically be better or easier, although it does help. And rushing around without first seeing what you are doing and why may give the impression of improving matters without actually changing anything: once the dust has settled, everyone returns to being the way they were.

In this society there is still a certain resistance to talking about emotions and motives, to exploring and understanding. When a relationship has broken down, or when someone is having problems that might have started in an unhappy past life, they often prefer not to rake over painful ashes by trying to work out why. This is a bit like believing that you should do nothing if you cut yourself. If you have a painful wound, it is tempting just to slap a plaster on and do nothing else, because opening up and cleaning the area would hurt so much. Of course, if that is what you did, the wound would fester and the end result would be far more dangerous and painful. The same goes for emotional wounds. It is only by facing up to what has happened that we can heal them and avoid repeating the same mistakes.

This book is written in the belief that 'raking over' the

distant and immediate past can only help you to make a better future. The idea is to give practical suggestions on how you can come to terms with your feelings, discuss them with the rest of your family, get support from family and friends, and make changes. We will introduce the techniques of discussion, negotiation and compromise and explain how anyone, even very young people, can take some control over their lives and make their voices heard, to make a second family a better one.

! ────────────────── *Task* ──────────────

Getting in the right frame of mind

Before you go any further, try this exercise to get you into a receptive frame of mind for constructive change.

Imagine a bird's nest, with an egg inside.

The egg is a fragile shell. It starts off as a beautiful object, shiny, round and perfect, until the bird is born. Then it cracks, breaks and is discarded, no longer useful.

The chick starts off as an ugly thing, a wet and bedraggled ball of fluff. But, as time passes, it grows into a fine and splendid creature.

The question to ask yourself is: do you see yourself as an egg or a chick ? Are you something that was once whole and complete but has been broken and ruined by the ending of your earlier relationships, or other painful experiences in your past, and can never be put back together again ? Or do you see yourself as something emerging from a hard time, who has to go through a period of feeling and looking rough before eventually blossoming once more ?

Think about which one you feel like, and consider why you might have felt like an egg, if that was the one you pictured yourself as being. You may think you're fated to be one rather than the other. In fact, you merely have to decide whether to see yourself as a winner or loser. Pick which one you want to be!

────────────────────────────────── !

___ ARE SECOND FAMILIES UNUSUAL ?___

> When someone says the word *family*
> a variety of vivid images and memories, attitudes and feelings
> always spring to mind.

What comes into your mind when someone mentions 'the family'?
The picture most of us have is of two adults, one male and one
female, married for the first time and living together, bringing
up their own children. We might add grandparents in the
background, and perhaps a cat and dog in the foreground, and set
them in a semi-detached house in the suburbs. Even if our own
family of origin had little resemblance to this description, we will
still tend to feel this is the norm. Furthermore, we are likely to
have strong feelings about the rightness or wrongness of this
image, and any other presented to us, because *family* is more than
just a description: the word itself has rich emotional associations.

When we say *family*, a variety of vivid images and
memories, attitudes and feelings invariably spring to mind.
Depending on your experience, these images may be of happiness
or of wretchedness, or a complex mixture of both. If we look
beyond what we would *prefer* family to mean, we might recognise
that families come in a far greater range of shapes and sizes than
2 adults + 2 children (+ 4 grandparents, 1 dog and 1 cat!). Cast an
eye over your neighbours, your friends and your relatives and
you'll soon see that very few families actually fit this idealised
picture. Yet most of us who live (as most of us *do* live) in
something different, still often feel that we are unusual. Shame at
being different and fear that nobody else could understand how
we feel frequently prevent us from sharing our difficulties and
asking for help when problems come along. So we get stuck with
a double load of distress: the problem itself, and the conviction
that it's a unique, impassable obstacle that's probably of our own
making.

FEELING DIFFERENT

When Henry and his second wife came for counselling, he recalled his own childhood. He remembered he'd always kept quiet about the fact that his mother had remarried, because he felt that this made him different from his friends.

My parents were divorced when I was eight and my mother took my three-year-old sister and me back to her home town where she married the man who had been her teenage sweetheart. He adored my sister, who became his little girl and soon forgot our father. I didn't. I didn't hate my step-father or anything. I could have liked him but I resented that he was there instead of my dad and he knew it and we never got on well. The real problem was that I had no one to talk to and I found it really hard to come to terms with my mixed-up emotions. Nobody in my school or my neighbourhood had a step-father, or so I thought, and I felt totally alone. I'm now in my forties, divorced, remarried with two children by my first wife, two by my second and four step-children, all living variously here, there and everywhere. I kept pretty quiet about the resultant problems until recently, when I went back to my home town and met up with some old schoolfriends and this subject came up. I couldn't believe it – my two best friends both said they'd been in exactly the same situation as I had been, and felt the same. For one, his parents had divorced and remarried when he was the same age as me, and the other's mother had died when he was five and his father had married again. Just like me, they had been convinced that everyone else's family (mine included!) was 'normal' while each of theirs had been the only weird one. After talking to you for the first time, I thought about all my friends and colleagues and asked the ones whose family set-up I didn't know about – you can ask about these sort of things nowadays ! The eye-opener was that not one, single person – not one – was untouched by this phenomenon. Every single one was either separated or divorced, with children in various combinations, or they came from step-families, or they had

*brothers or sisters or cousins or friends or somebody in this
situation. I used to think I was unique.*

Once Henry had realised he was neither unusual nor odd, he felt
able to ask for help. People who divorce and remarry or separate
from a long-term partner often suffer from the impression that
they are different. The image we still retain about relationships is
that there is only one Mr or Mrs Right for each of us and once we
have found ours, it is usual and normal to stay with them. This
simply isn't true. However unusual you may feel, the truth is that
second families are as old as any other family unit and are hardly
uncommon. Long before we kept written records, or even before
we painted on cave walls or engraved stone tablets, husbands or
wives would have died or otherwise been lost and new ones
would have taken their place.

A NORMAL FAMILY ?

> Only 1 in 20 households is a so-called 'typical' family:
> a breadwinner father and a stay-at-home mother
> bringing up their own two children.

Second families are neither new, nor are they particularly unusual,
since diversity is far more common than we like to admit. Around
150,000 couples divorce every year in England and Wales. One in
three of the 350,000 marriages each year is a remarriage for one or
both partners. At any one time, only 1 in 20 households is a so-
called 'typical' family of a breadwinner father and a stay-at-home
mother bringing up their own two children. Most of us at some
time pass through a stage of being in a family unit that fits into
this pattern, but the fact is that by the year 2000 only 50 percent of
young people will have spent their entire childhood in what many
of us still consider to be a 'normal' home life. And it is these ideas

of what is and is not normal that are really at the core of any problems in a second family. The relationships themselves may have inbuilt and inevitable difficulties, but much of the friction and tension comes about because a second family is operating in a world that still assumes that the traditional family is the norm. Second families *do* have inherent difficulties which we shall be looking at, but these difficulties are often caused or worsened by widely held prejudices. The main one, of course, is that the only unit in our society that can properly call itself a family is two adults married and living together, bringing up their own children.

The reality is that *family* is a much more elastic concept than this. A family can be two adults, married or unmarried, whose children have grown up and left them. It can be two adults of the same sex who have children. It can be two adults of the opposite sex who don't have children. Children living with a single parent whose partner has left or died, is a family. So is a single adult child caring for elderly parents. A family can also consist of two adults, married or unmarried, either or both of whom have had previous relationships ending in separation or divorce. They can be living full-time with children who are related by blood to only one, or caring part-time for children who stay at weekends or during school holidays. All these are just as much 'families' as the ideal stereotype.

A dictionary definition of family
is a group *nearly* connected by blood or *affinity*.

WHAT MAKES YOU DIFFERENT ?

When one or both of you have previously lived with another person, your relationship is just as normal and common as any other. But there are certain characteristics that can lead to problems. The main one is the very fact that one or both of you knows they are not the first person to have shared a home and a bed with the other. There are many occasions you may encounter in your life where you find yourself taking on responsibility once held by another person and stepping into someone else's shoes. You could be given a job which used to be done by someone else or move into a previously lived-in house. If something is not

! ================= *Task* =================

The problems you may start with

You may feel all of the dilemmas you encounter are the particular, unique problems found in a second family, with or without children. In fact, many are the same, common or garden disagreements anyone experiences in a new relationship or when there are adults and children around. Ask any member of a second family about the causes of the problems they experience, and the chances are that one or more of the following will be mentioned. Look at this list and add your own:

Jealousy
Fear of rejection
Fear of comparison
Money
Relatives and in-laws
Holidays and festivals, such as Christmas or Passover.

When there are children from the previous relationships, the following are also frequently mentioned. Can you add any more?

Difficulties in managing a divided lifestyle.
Important decisions about children, such as schooling.
Discipline.
Disagreements over contact.

!

brand-new, we often feel in the shadow of whatever or whoever was there before. You may find it uncomfortable to see the signs of their early occupancy and resent it when other people remark on how it used to be. You may find yourself deliberately changing things, not because they need changing but just to make your own mark.

But taking someone else's job or someone else's house cannot throw up the range of confused feelings, reactions and behaviour as becoming the partner, married or unmarried, of someone who has had an earlier significant relationship. And when this also involves taking on other people's children or having your own children accept into their lives an adult who is not their original parent, the difficulties can multiply. You may find that all the above feelings and reactions happen, but with very different consequences than just changing the wallpaper in your new house !

You may find it hard to face up to the feelings that really lie behind your arguments. Jan and Jed have been married for 13 years. In the first five years of their marriage they had frequent arguments that tended to happen when his first marriage was mentioned. The rows grew less frequent but they eventually realised that this was because they had each withdrawn from the other. When they came for counselling, each picked on different reasons for their disputes. Jed, who sees his children once a month and during school holidays, remembers arguments as mainly being about them:

Discipline was a major disagreement with us. I'm pretty easy-going and Jan likes to know what's what. Whenever Tom and Jesse came to stay, there were always big production numbers about manners at table and whether they cheeked her or not, and bedtimes and stuff like that. She wanted me to back her up, they'd say she had no right to tell them off and I felt stuck in the middle and really awkward. I mean, I only saw them one weekend a month. I wanted it to be fun, I wanted them to like coming to see me. The last thing I wanted to do was come down on them like some Victorian father reading the riot act.

Jan says the rows were, for her, about something closer to home.

I was jealous of his first wife, I admit it. If he mentioned her or said anything about their life together, I'd fly off the handle. She's really tall and slim and I'm short and I hated getting undressed in front of him – I thought he'd be thinking about her and wondering why he left her for me. I've always been a bit shy but I wasn't like this with anyone else.

It took Jan and Jed some time to recognise that their difficulties were really about their own relationship and their feelings about it being a second marriage for Jed. Whether it's money or decision-making, sex or children, or anything else that lights the touchpaper for your disputes, the reality is that none of these is the core problem. They're something to focus your disagreements upon. What actually causes problems is unfinished business left over from that first marriage. Second families have difficulties because of what they are and how they got there. Jan felt second-best because Jed had once loved someone else and every time his children came to stay, they only reminded her of this fact. Jed felt guilty about leaving his children and so walked on eggshells with them, but he also felt he didn't have what it takes to be a good husband, since he'd already failed once at that role. Both of them needed to take time to build up their own self-esteem and to value each other as husband and wife. Once their counsellor helped them to do this, they found they talked more but argued less.

STARTING A NEW RELATIONSHIP IN THE SHADOW OF AN OLD ONE

Starting a new relationship in the shadow of an old one has several drawbacks. One is how you may be feeling after the ending of the first relationship. Divorce or separation is considered to be the second most stressful life event you may experience, whether as the partner who is leaving, the one being left or as a child of the separating couple. Only a death is seen as more traumatic. In fact, studies have shown that losing a parent or partner through death is often far easier to cope with both in the immediate and the long-term than through divorce or separation. When a partnership ends in death, the obvious response of grief is accepted by everyone around you. There is a process, from disbelief through anger, pain and loss to eventual acceptance and renewal, which presents itself for us to follow and we are usually helped and supported in that journey by everyone we know. The break-up of a family is also something to mourn, but anger and accusation often complicate matters. Any chance of being able to go through the natural, gradual stages of mourning and emerge on the other side is often diminished, generally because everyone concerned is hampered with guilt and feelings of failure. We may also be held up by the incomplete nature of the situation. A death, after all, is a final and finite event, an ending that has clearly happened with a body to be buried or cremated and a person to be missed. In a divorce or separation, the missing person is still alive and walking around and the relationship may take some time to put to rest.

It is often hard to follow the healing process because of the common belief that if something goes wrong somebody must be 'to blame'. Most of us grow up with a nagging feeling that we don't quite meet the required standard, that we are to be found lacking. Young people in particular believe that their parents are faultless and that they themselves are always in the wrong. You may have been lucky enough to have grown up in a family with people who helped you to feel good about yourself, where you were praised for doing things well more than you were blamed for doing things badly, and you would have become someone who valued her or himself. If you were not, the chances are you would have grown up with a tendency to think it was your fault when

Reactions to loss

Reactions to a death and to the end of a relationship are almost identical. Losing someone is probably the most painful experience we can have. No one is surprised when we feel grief after a death. What is often not realised is that the death of a relationship we value is as disturbing as the death of a person we love. Getting over that relationship can take a long time. Realising how the experience might have affected you and how distressing it might have been can be helpful. When something or someone we value or are close to dies, we pass through several stages of grief. Because everyone's reaction to loss is individual, you may pass through the stages in a different order, and you may experience a particular stage more or less intensely than other people might. You may also find yourself dropping back into a stage you had left behind, or getting stuck in one. Have a look at these, and see if any of them describe the way you are, or have been, feeling:

Shock and disbelief. You may feel numb, be in a daze and not be able to take in what has happened. At this stage, people often say 'I don't believe it', 'This can't be happening', 'This doesn't make sense'.

Denial. You may refuse to accept your loss and carry on as usual, as if it hadn't happened. You may keep thinking the missing person is still there or be convinced they are about to walk in. You can feel cold and shivery as well as having a sensation of everything being rather 'unreal'. At this stage, people often say, 'It hasn't happened.'

Anger. You may feel violent emotions, towards the person who has gone, those left behind or towards yourself. You may feel restless, panic-stricken and anxious. At this stage, people often say, 'It was all so-and-so's fault!'

Bargaining. You may feel you could have done something to stop the loss and would be prepared to do anything to make it better now. At this stage, people often say, 'If only I hadn't . . .', 'If only I had . . . ', 'If I do such and such, perhaps things will be different'.

Depression. You may feel sad, hopeless and unable to raise the energy to do anything. At this stage, people often say, 'Nothing matters' or, 'I wouldn't care if I died tomorrow'.

Acceptance. As time passes, you will begin to come to terms with what has happened. You will again feel happy and whole. At this stage, people often say, 'I never thought I'd smile again, but I have!'

things went wrong. When a partnership breaks down, most of us are indeed quick to blame ourselves and feel we could have done better. Having said that, it's very human to point the finger of blame at someone else as quickly as possible, when we believe in our hearts of hearts that we are at fault. This is why the ending of a relationship, where two people who once loved each other move apart, can so quickly become a bitter, life-and-death battle.

Coping with loss and death

If you have been having a hard time adjusting to a new relationship, this may have something to do with how you or your partner have adjusted to the loss of your old one. How we cope with loss often depends on the sort of relationship we had and whether or not we knew what was about to happen. Six features make it more likely that you fare well or badly when a relationship ends, and in any subsequent family. Consider these descriptions and discuss with your partner whether any of them might apply to your situation.

What else is happening

Loss is made far worse if other major life changes come along at the same time. You are likely to find it particularly hard to cope if:

You move house

You change employment or schooling

Your income falls

Family festivals, such as Christmas or Passover, occur

You lose contact with other people, places or animals you also value

The sort of person you are

Your ability to cope with grief and loss changes at particular times in your life, and some people have more resilience. You are likely to weather a loss better if:

You have self-confidence and value yourself

You feel in charge of your life, not at the mercy of fate or luck

You are in good health

You are prepared to talk about your feelings

Support networks

Whether you cope with loss often depends on the presence of family and friends, your willingness to use the help they might offer, and their ability to offer the help you need. You are more likely to cope if:

Someone is there for you when you need them

Your supporters can listen and allow you to cry without trying to belittle your grief

Your supporters can put their own feelings, opinions and needs aside while listening to you

Sudden loss

Unexpected loss is far worse than having warning about what was going to happen. If your first family is broken up without warning, you may:

Not believe it has really happened and refuse to face up to the truth

Show immediate unhappiness and anxiety

Blame yourself and have a tendency to despair

Become isolated from friends and family

Keep thinking the lost partner is still there

Continue to feel lonely, depressed and fearful

Loss when the relationship was going badly

When you feel happy and thought the relationship was a good one, losing a partner can actually be easier to bear. Surprisingly, this is true even if you find out your partner did not seem to share your feelings, as when the loss happens because they leave you. When the relationship has been argumentative, the loss of someone you might not really regret losing can lead to:

Feeling fine at first but a keen sense of grief later

Lasting hope that the lost partner will come back

Feeling that the loss was your fault

Depression and ill-health

No confidence in yourself as a parent or a worker

When you can't do without them

When you have been unable to do the ordinary things of life without your partner's help, the reaction to loss is often to fall back into longing for the past. This can lead to:

Feelings of emptiness and insecurity

A sense of unreality

A longing for the lost partner to return

Loneliness and a feeling that the lost partner is still there

The conviction that it wouldn't matter if you were no longer alive

2

UNFINISHED BUSINESS

You may now be beginning to realise that there are solid reasons for the dilemmas facing you. The next question you might want to ask is, 'Can I do anything about this situation?' The first step may be to consider what bothers you in this relationship and why.

UNFINISHED BUSINESS

Divorce can be the end of a marriage and separation the end of a relationship but very rarely is the break a clean and complete one. Indeed, a clean break is never clean and rarely a break! When a relationship ends you can be left with feelings of failure, anger and bitterness, and have an overwhelming need to have these heard by your one-time partner. What often happens, however, is that both sides are so wrapped up in their own grief and bitterness that they cannot listen to what the other one is saying. This can leave each of you with the burden of being unheard. You may feel stuck with the wish to get those feelings out, to have your say and make the other person understand your emotions. You could then get locked into a continuing battle that can go on, often for an astoundingly long time after the relationship is supposed to have ended. Even when you start or are settled into a new relationship, that unfinished business can keep pulling you back, recalling old ties.

Difficulties in ending an old relationship and making a new family are increased by the fact that, up to now, our legal system has made divorcing couples into adversaries. Instead of being encouraged to sit down together to settle and finish disagreements and to work together for everyone's best interests, the system pits both partners against each other. This often puts them on a runaway course to spite and revenge. It is hardly surprising that the aftermath of a divorce or separation is frequently anger and bitterness, low self-esteem and a lack of self-confidence in both partners. Trying to build a new family on such shaky foundations, while dealing with problems left over from the old one, is far from easy. When everyone seems to expect you to make adjustments quickly and to be able to deal with what has happened the difficulties are even greater.

Ali visited a counsellor because he and his new wife were having problems. Ali married Romily a year after he went through a bitter and angry divorce from his first wife. He said they have a good relationship and love each other but he had confessed to still thinking of his ex, and she found this confusing and hurtful. He feels guilty and regrets the way his first marriage ended, with a bitter fight in court over money.

My mother and Romily think the whole thing is just past and gone, over and done with. But we were together for four years and while Romily is the one I love, you can't just sweep four years of your life away like that. I need a bit of time but they won't let me have it. The odd thing is that when we row, I sometimes find myself saying things to hurt Romily that aren't really about her – such as saying she's mean with money, which is the last thing she is. The person I'm really talking about is my ex-wife, not her.

Unable to resolve the arguments he never finished in his old relationship, Ali is trying to resolve them in his new one. Unfortunately, Romily would only come to one session of counselling and left saying that she would only come back if Ali and the counsellor promised not to talk about his first marriage. She didn't want to see what the past had to do with their problem and this meant that little could be done. Many couples, however, find that looking back can help them to put their difficulties into perspective. They can then focus on the strengths that can be found in any relationship, if you are prepared to look for and enhance them.

YOU AND YOUR PARTNER

You may think that any disagreements or difficulties you and a new partner are having are your fault or the relationship's fault. You may find that any problems you are having overshadow the positive side of your relationship. In fact, it is likely to be leftover aspects of the past that could be affecting you, and the situation rather than the people involved that might be to blame. Use the following exercise to start working out what upsets you and why, and to strengthen the plus points.

This feeling of not yet having drawn a line and ended what there was between you, of perhaps not even having your feelings admitted to, let alone heard or understood, means that you may continue to feel connected to your former partner. This may be true even when you have no children to link you together – to require you to go on being in touch and to give a visible reminder that once there was something between you.

STARTING AGAIN

Even the happiest first-time relationships seldom start with a completely clean sheet. Events in your childhood or teenage years may affect your ability to make a happy and lasting relationship. Your past casts a shadow over your present and your future. Your relationships in childhood – with parents and with siblings – leave you with hopes and expectations for your adult intimate partnerships. But second-time families have all the baggage anyone brings to a relationship and the after-effects of the ending of a committed first relationship. Most second families come together in the shadow of a breakdown in a former relationship,

! ═══════════════ *Task* ═══════════════

When a relationship has hit a sticky patch, every little annoyance can blow up into a stand-up row. The trick is to save disputes for the important things – and to make those fights constructive discussions rather than conflicts. Work out your priorities. What are the things you seriously dislike? What are the things that just get on your nerves? And what are the things you actually like? You can see them as the three colours of a traffic light. Red is the STOP sign; something you'd really like your partner to change. Yellow is WARNING; something that puts you on edge, that they should be aware about. And Green is GO; something you really like and they might think about doing more, as a way of getting the balance right. Get a sheet of paper and three colour pens – red, yellow and green. Make three columns with these headings using the appropriate colours:

THINGS THAT ANGER:

THINGS THAT ANNOY:

THINGS THAT PLEASE:

Fill in the columns and talk over what you've written. Why do these come to mind? Can you think about earlier times when these things have pleased or annoyed you? What does it remind you of when your partner does them?

Think of your relationship as a piggy bank. Each time you have a row – and make an entry in the red or yellow column – you take a coin out. If you're forever taking out, pretty soon the bank is empty and you have nothing left. But every time you put a coin in – by making an entry in the green column – you fill up the bank. Having disputes does less harm to a relationship if you keep filling the bank as well as taking away. !

and with the living presence of the former partner still looming over them. Statistics suggest second marriages are even more likely than first marriages to end in divorce.

> It isn't the fact that yours is a second partnership that makes the difference, but whether or not you free yourself from the after-effects of your previous partnership and its ending.

However much you may think or hope that a second marriage or partnership may be a new start, it is impossible to make past relationships, and the experiences you shared, disappear. Even when a new partner and a chance for a new family set-up comes along, it may be very difficult to break away from the memories

Task

Finishing the argument

If you and your new partner are to make a successful relationship, it is vital to put your feelings about any previous relationships to rest. This is partly to separate any feelings of annoyance, irritation or anger for your present partner from leftover feelings from the past, and partly to draw a line under the emotional link between you and your earlier partner so that you can focus on the present one. If you are still seeing your ex because you have children and need to be in contact, ask him/her to join you in some sessions with a mediator or counsellor. If, for any reason, you cannot have this meeting in reality, have it in your imagination. Imagine your ex is sitting in a chair in front of you and tell them everything you want them to know. Or write it down in a letter, even if you never send it. Once off your chest, you may find you can face the new relationship afresh.

or the patterns of the old one. This is as true of a relationship that ended when the other person left you as it is of one you chose to leave, or were glad ended. Whatever the circumstances of a new relationship, memories, habits and therefore comparisons with the old one may come up, and get in the way. What often happens is that ex-partners continue to quarrel and wrangle, and in spite of the new relationship carry on as if they are still connected. Or, new partners import their feelings about the old ones into the new relationship and behave as they did with the previous partners. New partners often get sucked into the arguments between exes. Indeed, they often take over the hostile role while their partner lets go of their own anger and sits back. This is why new partners should resist being involved in the arguments of former partners. If they have business still to finish, it's theirs to sort out and no reflection on you.

TALKING IT OVER AND BREAKING THE CYCLE

Any blended family must rise from the ashes of a tragedy and a death – the death of a partner or the death of a relationship. Facing up to and resolving this together is far more likely to result in a better future. You can't and shouldn't try to sweep what has happened before under the carpet. Second marriages are at a higher risk of ending in divorce and this may be partly because we rush in looking for a better future, refusing to look back at what may still affect us from the past. We can often get stuck in futile disagreements that never seem to be resolved. No argument is as bad as the repetitive argument that goes nowhere, where you feel the other person isn't listening to you, or that he or she is simply nagging. If you find this is happening, either with ex partners or your present one, there are ways of calling a halt to the process and of putting these old arguments to rest.

What is the very worst scenario you can imagine in your new relationship? Continued arguments, perpetual disagreements, sustained hostility? Whatever your situation at the moment, the fact is that by doing nothing, you are probably encouraging your fears to materialise. By taking action, however painful, you could have the opportunity to direct matters. Taking the initiative is at the core of any successful relationship. Don't listen to the myths that say tinkering with it only makes it worse. That may be true of clocks, but not of relationships! There are a number of practical actions you could take that might contribute to a stress-free second family.

Being able to communicate effectively is not an art we are born with but a skill we need to learn. It's an appalling fact that most of us have had very little chance of learning something as important as how to communicate properly. We don't learn to do so at school, and often we don't learn communication skills from our parents. So it is something you may have to practise and perfect as an adult. If you want somebody to listen to what you are saying, you have to offer them the exchange of listening to what they are saying. Communication is not just a question of getting people to listen to you, it has to be two-way. Many people think making themselves understood is the same thing as getting their own way, and this may be one reason we refuse to listen to the other person's side of the argument. We think that if we do hear them out, the chances are they might 'win'. But proper communication doesn't lead to just one person's ideas being taken on wholesale. On the contrary, it leads to negotiation where everyone has their say and is heard and a final solution is found which satisfies everybody to some extent. An important point to note is that after negotiation you may not get precisely what you want, but because everyone gets part of what they want you are all encouraged to go along with the final decision.

! ======================== *Task* ========================

Having a constructive argument

There's nothing wrong with having a disagreement. The problems arise when it just leads to shouting, anger and further confusion. If someone is being accused of nagging, a common complaint in arguments, the chances are that their request is not being heard, either because the other person doesn't want to hear, they aren't making themselves clear or because the real demand is concealed. The trick is to make sure you are being heard and that you make yourself clear.

Sit down with your partner. Agree a set time for your discussion, so that you will spend the next 30 minutes or whatever talking it over together. Or, agree to talk until both of you think you have arrived at some conclusion. Use a clock to make sure both of you get an equal share of speaking and being heard, and listening. Agree, too, to these guidelines:

When you talk about what is bothering you, you have to say 'I'. It's supposed to be arrogant or selfish to use the 'I' word so we tend to avoid it. When we want to make a point, in discussion or argument, we either claim 'everyone' or 'all my friends' or 'your mother' thinks so and so, rather than taking responsibility for those feelings ourselves. Or we put the responsibility on the other person, by saying 'You make me think or do such and such'. One important step to constructive argument is owning, or taking responsibility for, our own feelings. So, using 'you', 'one', 'they', 'everyone' – in fact anything except 'I' is outlawed. There is a great difference in saying 'I'm angry because when you talk about your past I feel second best to your ex' instead of 'You make me feel second best!'. The main difference is that the other person may rightly object to the second statement because it may not be their intention at all, and once they disagree you will find yourself stuck in the circular argument. But no one can disagree with an honest explanation of your own feelings. And once they are explained, you may be well on your way to dealing with them.

Confront problems, not people. When you feel upset, stop to work out exactly what is bothering you. Instead of shouting at the person, explain what your anger or distress is really about, then find a way of agreeing on a solution.

Accept that you can't help what you feel, only what you do about it. As we have already discussed, anyone in a second family is likely to have a complex and mixed range of feelings about themselves, the other people involved and the situation. Perhaps one of the most important messages we need to take on board is that those feelings, however destructive they are and however much they may distress you, are likely to be natural and normal. If you want to become comfortable with yourself and to reach a working arrangement with everyone else, the first step is to recognise and understand why you feel the way you do. So accept your feelings, even if they are sometimes feelings you would rather not have. Be honest about what you are feeling and why. You are not to blame for your *emotions*.

Accept that you are, however, in control of the *actions* you take because of your emotions. You're being dishonest if you say you can't help what you might do. Having gained some insight into why a second family might be so difficult, you can pinpoint your own fears, angers or anxieties and come to understand how the other people involved might feel, and then work on strategies for making a change. Sometimes a 'pre-emptive strike' can nip problems in the bud. Many eventually happy second families start off badly or go through difficult periods, so don't despair. There are many things you can all do to improve your life together.

STRESS AND ITS EFFECTS

What may also get in the way of developing and strengthening new partnerships can be the exhausting after-effects of having gone through a stressful time, in the previous few months or even

!────────────────*Task*────────────────

Stress ratings

Life events always mean a certain amount of stress. Stress isn't, in itself, necessarily a bad thing. It can boost your energy and be a stimulus to action. But unmanaged stress can affect your health by obstructing your body's ability to fight illness. Two psychologists, Thomas Holmes and Richard Rahe, developed a system of measuring common experiences that were stressful. Happy events could be as stressful as unhappy ones. They listed typical life events, scored in Life Change Units (LCUs). They found that anyone scoring more than 300 points in a year was at an 80 per cent risk of suffering physical or emotional illness. A score of 200 to 300 puts you at a 50 per cent risk. Looking at this list, and remembering that an event need not have *happened* in the last year still to *affect* you, what is your score?

LIFE EVENT	LCU
Death of partner	100
Divorce	73
Marital separation	65
Death of close family member	63
Illness or injury	53
Getting married	50
Change in health of family member	44
Pregnancy	40
Sex difficulties	39
New family member	39
Change in financial state	38
Death of close friend	37
Change in number of rows with partner	35
Taking on a mortgage or loan	31
Son or daughter leaving home	29
Trouble with in-laws	29
Change in living conditions	25
Change in work hours or conditions	20
Change in residence	20

Change in schools	20
Change in social activities	18
Change in number of family get-togethers	15
Change in eating habits	15
Holiday	13
Christmas	12
YOUR TOTAL	

! ——————————— *Task* ———————————

A quiet space

Couples and individuals going through a stressful period in their lives often find it hard to take time to relax. There can be so many pressing demands on your time and attention that it seems selfish or unreasonable to concentrate on your own needs. You might feel that you are being self-indulgent or you may simply be unable to switch off and take 'time out'. Here's a relaxation technique that you could try out, to give you a chance to unwind. It only takes a few moments but allows you to rest and refresh yourself in a surprisingly quick time. Try it in the evening, before going to sleep, while having a coffee or lunch break . . . or whenever you can.

Sit comfortably, or lie down. Close your eyes and imagine somewhere quiet and tranquil you'd like to be – on a seashore, in a forest, in a meadow. It may be somewhere you've actually been or somewhere you only know about from films or photographs. Picture the way it looks, the way it sounds, the way it smells. Imagine yourself walking through this scene and then just sitting down to enjoy the setting in peace. When you are ready to leave, count slowly from one to 10 and then imagine yourself getting up and walking back to where you are. Open your eyes again.

The more often you do this, the easier it becomes to 'be' in your ideal spot and the more relaxed you will be when you come away from it.

!

the past few years. We often forget exactly how much stressful events affect us.

STOCKTAKING

What happened before your present relationship does not have to blight your future. Past events can leave you with the experience and the resolve to make a happier, more satisfying and successful family life for yourself and others, the second time around. Sometimes, a desire to use a second partnership to heal all the wounds of your former life can be problematical. On the negative side, you can load too much of a burden on to your new partner and the relationship, expecting them and it to be the answer to all your grief. But on the positive side, having a second chance can

! ============================ *Task* ============================

Taking stock

Before you go any further, you might want to discuss how you feel about developing or continuing in this second relationship. If you feel there are problems, what are they? Sit down with you partner and, with your present situation in mind, fill in as many ideas as you can under these two headings:

           THINGS I'VE LOST   THINGS I'VE GAINED

For every item you put in the first column, you should add one to the other. If the left-hand column is easier to fill in than the other, you may need to work hard at this relationship, or even consider abandoning it. Or, it may bring home to you all the good things you've got to give to each other.   !

enable you not only to make this new relationship work but also to redress some of the damage you and others around you might have suffered before. The key to making it work is examining what is going on and why. Facing up to painful aspects of your life and your relationship is often hard but it may well be worth it. Stocktaking means looking at what the problems are, what your strengths are and what solutions could work for you.

MAINTAINING THE COUPLE
RELATIONSHIP

A second family will always involve dilemmas that will need to be addressed. But however desperate you may feel and however insoluble those problems may seem, there will be a way to cope. You can change the way you act or change the way you feel and either or both will alter the situation. If you are prepared to put some effort into becoming aware of potential problem areas, understanding how they could affect all involved and doing something about them, the results could be rewarding for all concerned.

One important aspect to keep in mind is that a second family is always about a couple relationship. You wouldn't be where you are if you and your partner did not wish to live and love together. Whether there are children in your new partnership or you are on your own as a couple, it is vital to make time for your personal relationship. Second relationships often suffer because they're established at stages in our lives when we may have less time for ourselves. First relationships tend to develop while we have fewer responsibilities. We may still be in education or in the early phase of our working life. We have fewer family ties, so we can devote more time and attention to the person we're attracted to and soon love. But second families tend to come when there are other claims on us. The problem then is that we can easily be distracted from putting in the care and attention that is needed to maintain a relationship. Whatever else may be going on in your life, it's very important to drop everything else every now and then, to make each other feel special.

! ———————————— *Task* ————————————

Treat yourself

Take time out for yourself, as a couple. Make a date – once a month or, better still, once a week – to do something together. Set aside some time which will be for you two on your own and don't let anything get in the way. You could use this to treat each other to some pampering, at home. Give each other a massage or a foot rub or take a bath together and scrub each other's backs. Sit and listen to some music, read or watch a programme on television that will get you talking. Or you could go out on your own, for a meal, for a drink or if you can't afford that, for a walk. If you have children, get a baby-sitter or arrange with friends or family to give you a break so nothing can interrupt your private time.

!

PART TWO
WHEN THERE ARE CHILDREN

3

A TIE TO THE PAST

It is often said that when a couple make love in the privacy of their own bedroom, there are actually six people present; the couple themselves and, in spirit, both sets of parents! When you go to bed with a new partner and one or both of you has had a previous, significant relationship, the chances are that your ex partners and even *their* parents join the imaginary audience. When one or both of you has had children in a previous relationship, all of your children are also invisible, critical and daunting spectators. And not just in bed. In the kitchen, bathroom and living room, you are under scrutiny and up for judgement. If a second relationship has its difficulties, there is no doubt these are made more noticeable if not more acute when there are children involved.

The very existence of children from a former relationship continually serves to remind members of both the old and the new partnership of the unfinished nature of the former association. When there are children, there is no way round the fact that although the separated couple are no longer husband and wife or partner and partner, they are both still parents. Neither can completely turn their back on the past and begin again; their children are an invisible chain still tying them together. Children are also, all too often, a channel through which arguments left over from the relationship can continue to be played out. As far as a second family is concerned, perhaps the main problem is that the existence of that parental link prevents you from ever totally turning over a new leaf.

Whether you have children or not, developing a second

relationship in the shadow of the past can be struggle. But when either or both of you have that tangible reminder, 'left over' from the last time, problems tend to become more obvious. These can start right at the beginning of your new relationship. Trying to establish a new relationship when one or both of you have children is anything but easy.

WHEN DO YOU INTRODUCE THE CHILDREN?

In some second relationships, that there are children from the previous partner is a known fact from the start. But in others, when the couple meet it is as if they are both single – perhaps friends introduce them or they meet at a party or at a disco or bar – nobody thinks to mention that there are children, or they may get to know each other at work without being aware of each other's home circumstances. It may take some time before the existence of children emerges. One of you may assume the other knows, and so not think to underline this or talk about it. Or you may choose not to mention for some time that you have children, and the longer you leave it, the more awkward it may be. Patti and Tyrone asked for help because she still felt angry, a year later, after discovering that he had two children, something he had kept from her for the first year she knew him.

He sees them one evening in the week and one day with an overnight stay on the weekend. I would see him most, but not every, night in the week and he'd take me out over the weekend, sometimes Saturday and sometimes Sunday. He said he had family he had to see but I never realised he meant children until we were getting really serious and talking about moving in together, when he had to come clean. It was a shock, I have to tell you. I was angry with him at first for not telling me but then I had to admit I can't see how or when it might have been easy to say. I might have been put off getting to know him if I'd known what I was taking on. But I was hurt, I felt he hadn't trusted me.

If children come to stay with one of you on a part-time basis, or spend some of their time with the other parent, you may, like Tyrone, be able to keep their existence secret for some months. Like him, you may find the juggling and deception involved emotionally and physically draining. He says:

I began to feel as if I was having another woman on the side. Making up excuses was hard, not just keeping my story straight but feeling bad about keeping Patti in the dark. I never directly lied to her, but not being straight felt as if I was.

Tyrone felt guilty for not coming clean with Patti, but felt he had had no alternative. She could see his point and because of that, felt unable really to tell him the depth of her hurt and anger, with the result that it kept bursting out in rows about other matters. They needed help because they found they'd have a searing row every week. Once they talked it through and she could face up to her hidden feelings, they realised the rows always came two days after a visit, when Patti's feelings could be contained no longer. Once she had had the opportunity to really let loose in one, massive session of shouting, crying and explaining how she felt, Patti and Tyrone could settle down afresh with the fact that he had two children.

CHILDREN IN SECOND FAMILIES

> If there are children, whether they live with you or not your relationship cannot simply be one-to-one.

Problems do not end when both of you know about any children you might have. If there are children, at some point you will have to face up to the fact that whatever happens between you, it

cannot simply be a one-to-one situation. Whether the children live
with you, see you frequently or occasionally or even if there is no
contact, their presence affects you. This means that your
relationship has a significant aspect, from the beginning. You are
not only a couple, you are also members of a stepfamily. You may
have to contend with everyday practical problems, such as
having to get a baby-sitter if you want to go on a date or trying to
get some privacy when there are children in the house. Or you
may have to make choices between seeing the children or the new
partner. Then there are the decisions you'll have to make about
social events – which ones do you want to attend alone as a
couple and which do you want to share with your children? Will
you or won't you go on holiday together? If so, with or without
the youngsters? There are also the emotional difficulties of
dealing with your feelings and theirs about sharing lives.

One of the main stumbling blocks to forming a second family
when there are children involved is the fact that children come as
part of the package. They predate the couple rather than the other
way round. In most families, the couple have the opportunity to
establish their relationship for some time before children come
along. In stepfamilies, they are already there. The problems of
trying to create a solid foundation to your new relationship with
children around are often such that it is tempting to keep the kids
right out of it. This may seem sensible, in practical terms. The
drawback is that the children may feel rejected, unwanted or
angry at having something going on behind their backs, and will
make their feelings known sooner or later.

In first-time families, the couple develop their own way of
dealing with each other and learn to live together before children
come on the scene. Once children do arrive, adults and children
grow together, learning each other's characters as they also learn
their respective roles of parent and child. The reverse is true in a
second family. The relationship between the new adult and child
has no time to develop before being seen as a full-blown 'parent
and child' relationship. Furthermore, rather than having some

choice over whether or not to fill your lives and your home with children, you may feel this becomes something beyond your control. Neither new adult nor child has a say in the existence of the other and both come to the arrangement with personalities already formed and unknown to the other. Even if the new partner is aware that they are taking on the package deal of adult and children, it may still be difficult actually to anticipate what life is going to be like until quite late on in the proceedings. What may be expected, what may be wanted out of family life, may not only be different from what you had imagined, but dramatically conflicting, particularly if this is going to be an occasional arrangement and the children will live elsewhere full-time, or if the children are going to split their time equally between households.

POINTS OF VIEW

Part of the problem with second families with children is that there are so many conflicting needs. During a first-time courtship the only people you really have to be concerned about apart from yourselves might be your parents. Relationships develop slowly and gradually and the transition from 'dating' to 'courting' to 'living together' to 'planning a future' may be hard to pin down. You proceed at your own pace, in the knowledge that your plans will have little or no bearing on the day-to-day life of others. When there are children involved, their feelings and their well-being have to be considered. They may demand answers before you are ready to give them and behave in ways that affect what you do and how and when you do it.

Jean avoided telling her two children that Barry was going to be living with them until he had actually moved in.

We all got on well, or so I thought, and it just seemed wrong to make a big announcement about it. And anyway, I didn't feel I needed to ask their permission for what I decided was for the best.

So I put it off until one day Tracy suddenly said, 'Is Barry living here for good, or what?'. I said yes and that was about it. I told them we were getting married a few weeks later and it was even harder than I thought, because they stared at the wall and pretended not to hear what I had said, and then Tracy said, 'Well, he can't tell us what to do because he's not my father', and that was that. Pretty soon Stevie was acting up, getting in with a bad crowd, and Tracy was in trouble at school. They were rude to both of us and the atmosphere at home went from bad to worse.

Barry and Jean felt they had got off on the wrong foot and that, once spoiled, the situation could never be put right. They did spend some time talking with a counsellor, but were pessimistic about any suggestions for change. They felt powerless themselves to do anything and met each plan that was discussed with an objection. They did take home some schemes for ways of talking and of making changes in their behaviour, but stopped coming to counselling soon after.

> Children of separated parents will always harbour the hope
> that their parents will get back together again.

Couples who have divorced or separated are often right in thinking that children will always harbour the hope that their parents will get back together again, however unreasonable or even undesirable this may be, and this is one of the reasons for the stress and tension you may feel when a new relationship develops. The announcement that the new person is not just a passing fancy temporarily taking the place of the estranged parent but a permanent partner can cause enormous anger and pain to children. Marriage or living together with a new partner is the final statement that the relationship between the ex-partners really is over for good, and it may be resisted strenuously. The fact that the new adult may be tolerated or even liked by the child will not stop children hoping that their parents will be reconciled. Paul, for instance, got on well with his father James's second partner Deirdre and it was clear that he had no wish to have her eliminated from the equation. But that didn't stop him hoping that his parents might get together again in some way.

He hated the fact that James and Laura lived in different homes, let alone different cities. He often used to talk about all of us living together – Laura, himself, James and me. He never really explained how he thought this would have worked but I have the feeling he had an elaborate plan for an extended house with quarters for her, quarters for us and a sort of free-flowing access for himself, his cat and ours. It actually would have been an ideal solution in many ways and I wish we'd had the chance to try it. In fact, I think the worst problems would have been getting the cats to accept each other!

LIFE STAGES

The isolation felt by many people, both when a family breaks up and when it re-forms, can be a direct result of the belief that 'family' has only one correct structure and anything else is out of step. It can also be a reflection of the natural progression that we all make through life, which can be described as 'Life Stages'.

> The roles of parent and newly-wed
> do not sit easily together.

Individuals, marriages and families all go through a natural progression from beginning, middle to end. As an individual, you pass from babyhood to toddlerhood, from pre-school to childhood, from adolescence to young adult, from growing adult to full adult, and then on to parenthood, maturity, mid-life and old age.

Marriages and families go through exactly the same stages. Life Stages broadly correspond to age, so while you are a child, a teenager or a single adult most of your friends are your peer group, in the same state. Once you get married or live with someone for a reasonable time, your friends are also couples. This is either because all of you are at an age or time in life when you go through the same stage, or because you gravitate towards other people in the same position. Married couples or long-term partners, especially those with children, seldom have single friends. Possibly this is because you drift away and have less in common when you can't share the same concerns of married life and parenthood. Another explanation is a sense of discontinuity, of 'wrongness' felt by people trying to retain a friendship across life stages. When some of you are at one stage and others at another, the feeling is that you don't have enough shared experiences or understanding in common to get on with each other. Even though you may be of similar ages, other factors put you in a different pigeon-hole in the Life Stage progression. Separation and family break-up can catapult you out of the comfortable slot you were in and remarriage can put you back in one that may not fit. The adult who once considered him or

! ================= *Task* =================

Look at this table, showing the Life Stages with a brief description of what tends to happen to you during each stage. You can see that becoming a partner in a settled relationship and becoming a parent tend to coincide with particular points in your individual Life Stages. If you are in, or considering, a second family, you may find your Marital and Parental Life Stages no longer match up to the diagram. Which stages have you passed through? Which Stages are you in now, or can see yourself entering soon? Are you jumping forward, or back, across Life Stages? Discuss with your partner how you feel and how you think this may affect you.

LIFE STAGES

Personal Life	Married Life	Parental Life
1 *Baby* Discover own body as separate from mother.		
2 *Child* Move outside home and learn values and rules.		
3 *Adolescent* Explore sexuality and own identity.		
4 *Young adult* Establish life style and home away from parents.		
5 *Courtship/ Marriage* Develop loving relationship and balance being an individual with being a couple.	*New couple* Beginning of a shared life.	
6 *Parenting* Adjust to accepting children into your life.	*Having babies* Loss of private one-to-one life.	*Beginners* Baby takes up full attention.
7 *Early mid-life* Balance own need with children's.	*Raising children and adolescents* Challenges to your own time together.	*Full-time* Accept child growing up
8 *Later mid-life* Accept achievements in life coming to a halt.	*Adjusting to your children's adulthood* Accept more time together.	*Becoming in-laws and then grandparents* Accept children making own relationships.
9 *Retirement* End of working life and approach of old age.	*The 'empty nest'* A lone couple again. Adjust to returning to life as it was.	*Grandparents* Adjust to new demands.
10 *Old age* Accept illness and death around the corner.	*Partner dies* Accept ending of marital life.	

!

herself to be primarily a parent may now see him or herself primarily as a newly-wed – roles that do not sit easily together and which may conflict.

This conflict was felt by Paula who divorced after 10 years of marriage and five years later married Scott, who was 18 years older than her.

My two were 12 and 10 but Scott had three grown-up children. Then, we had our own baby and we both found it very confusing. His friends obviously thought he was mad having a baby and going through the nappies and teething bit again and his children – who had children of their own – simply didn't know whether they should act like brothers and sisters or uncles and aunts. My two were riven with embarrassment and my mother was, too. My friends were fine with me, because two of them were having children too, but they didn't know how to behave with Scott and kept treating him like an indulgent grandfather rather than a father. It was all very odd!

BIRDS OF A FEATHER

Whether we realise it or not, many of us have pretty firm ideas about who should marry whom. We tend to feel that 'birds of a feather flock together'. Partners who are dissimilar – for instance, coming from a different race or with very different backgrounds – may find friends and family unsupportive, critical or even openly against them. This feeling that you have crossed the line of who properly goes with whom can also come up when a couple marries or sets up home and by doing so crosses these 'Life Stages'. An example would be when a single person marries someone who has already been married and has a family. There may be an unspoken feeling that one of you is selling yourself short and the other is unfairly getting somebody of a higher status than they deserve. This happened to Kerry, who met George on holiday in Italy with his three children. They fell in love, continued to see each other when they returned home and married three months later.

I was totally unprepared for the naked hostility shown by his family, his parents, brother and sisters, and many of his old friends. I was 22 at the time, just started on my first job and he was a successful businessman with a large house and these three children, who were all delightful. But the message I got from everyone else was that I was a gold digger – why else would I be marrying a man 15 years older than me? I was made to feel a total slut and they treated him as if he'd just lost his head and they hoped he'd come to his senses soon. We had a party for me to meet his friends and for them to meet me. It was a total disaster. They treated me like a servant or something he'd picked up for the night and at the end of it, when they'd all gone, we sat down and howled with laughter at the way they'd behaved because if I hadn't laughed I'd have cried.

When a relationship changes through separation, divorce or because of a death, you may find that old friends, even best friends, might abandon you or cool off. Friends can find the single state alarming and even fear that it is a 'catching' condition. After all, the same-sex member of the couple may be tempted to copy their friend and become a free agent again, while the opposite sex one may be tempted to have an affair! This avoidance is not only because they are thinking of themselves and their own relationships. We often avoid someone who is going or has gone through a difficult or depressing time because we don't feel able to help them and may even make things worse for them. The fear is that it would look silly not to mention what has happened but that if we do talk about it, the tears will start. We'll then feel guilty at having made them upset and we won't know what to say.

Friends may then be delighted when a new relationship starts because it restores the balance. You may find yourself coming under extreme pressure 'not to rock the boat' – not to voice any reservations. The hope is that the new couple and any children will have found a 'happily-ever-after', and be part of the group again. If what is really going on is not quite by the anticipated script, friends and relatives may ignore all the signs or even say you are being silly if you try to express them. Some or all of those concerned may then feel that they have to pretend to their friends or people outside the home that the relationships within are happy. The pretence may not only be for other people's benefit. We may try to fool ourselves as well and insist that all is well when we know that there are some problems that have not been tackled.

When Sophie's daughter Samantha remarried, taking her son and daughter to live with Bob and his two sons, she ignored many signs of discontent because she was so keen for her daughter to find some happiness.

I was so pleased because Sam had a very bad time with her first husband, who was unfaithful and a brute. Bob seemed so nice and his children were charming and polite. I suppose I rather went overboard, telling her how lucky she was and doing all I could to help them set up house together. She says she tried to talk to me at the time but I don't remember. I don't think I heard her or was willing to hear her. When it finally all came out, that he mistreated her, too, and his boys bullied my grandchildren, I was so shocked and so surprised. And I felt awful because she put up with it for four years before she told anyone. She said it started from little beginnings but nothing was ever said and she felt unable to talk about it, and that was why it went from bad to worse.

Ignoring warning signs often comes from having a strong belief about how we would like a family to be. This may not be harmful in itself since aspirations are fine to have as goals. The problems come when we refuse to see the reality, set up fantasies and insist that they rule our lives and actions, even when such insistence begins to create difficulties. There are two contradictory myths that hinder making good relationships a second time around. The first is that everything in the garden is lovely. If this is your second partnership, when you tell friends and relatives that you are remarrying, you may find yourself the subject of a sustained campaign of gooey sentimentality. This happened to Michael whose wife died of cancer at the age of 37 leaving him with a three-year-old daughter and a four-year-old son.

We managed, although the first year was really hard. I had grief to deal with as well as coming to terms with being a full-time single dad and all that that entailed. I'd known Josie for years – she was a school friend of Tina, my first wife. When so many of my friends found excuses not to be there, she was like a rock and it seemed inevitable that we should get together eventually. What we hadn't prepared for when we decided to get married was the way everyone popped out of the woodwork again, all cooing like doves about how wonderful it all was. She was told by some of her friends that she must be pleased because she'd skipped the nappy and vomit stage of babies and gone straight into the cutesie toddler bit. Which was pretty insensitive because Josie has always wanted a baby of her own, and still does. I got the full treatment about what a relief it must have been for me to have help again and the kids kept getting told they must be pleased to have a mother again. They were seven and eight by that time and no, they weren't pleased at all. They liked Josie but the last thing they wanted her to be was their mum, for all sorts of reasons. Dealing with all those reasons was made extra hard by the stuff we were getting thrown at us.

In fairy stories, the hero and heroine always live happily-ever-after, just like that. In real life, good relationships take planning, effort and, most important, awareness and insight. If you are going to take on the emotion-laden task of making a new relationship out of the ashes of an old one, you need at least to acknowledge that this is what you are doing. Permitting any reservations on your or your partner's part to be buried or pushed

aside will not make your lives any easier. Members of a second
family often cling, desperately and with mounting despair, to the
belief that everything must be fine simply because they actually
suspect that the second myth is the truth – that a second
relationship, especially when there are children around, is doomed
from the start.

> Children may be a painful reminder to their parent of a bitter
> or unhappy liaison or a jealous reminder to a new partner
> that someone was there before.

Children and their parents will often have a very different view
about the end of one relationship and the beginning of another.
Often the circumstances that create a second family are hedged
about with tragedy, bitterness, anger, or feelings of failure. In
addition, children will almost certainly have loyalties and often
mixed feelings towards the other natural parent – including
anger, loss and guilt – and these may not be understood but show
up in bad behaviour or unhappy feelings. This makes it all the
more difficult for you to talk about any anxieties or seek any help.

Central to many of the problems in blended families is the
assumption we make, as adults, that parents and children share a
common viewpoint when it comes to looking at the break-up of
the old and the formation of the new family. Nothing could be
further from the truth. When you and a partner separate, you are
at the end of a process – the process of your partnership coming
apart. Your children, however, are at the beginning of one – the
process of their family disintegrating. When you enter into a new
relationship, it is a beginning for you. But for the children it may
be an end – the end of their family and life as they have known it.

The needs of children are often felt to be the most important
consideration in any family. Most parents put their children first
when making decisions and planning. But when the family breaks
up and a new one forms, the brutal truth is that it is the adults'

needs that are in front. Children may find themselves drawn in, as spectators or participants, to the problems and feelings of their parents in a way that is beyond their experience and understanding. Children can find being faced with this profoundly disturbing, and their reactions and your expectations can lead to all sorts of difficulties. You may feel you know what is best for your family. You may need to recognise that what is best for you is not always best for your children and may certainly not be what they think is best for themselves.

Divorce and separation are an adult's solution to their
own problems.
Remarriage is a choice made by adults for adults.

GETTING RID OF THE PAST

Many couples struggling to develop a new relationship while coping with children from another partnership feel strongly that if only there were no contact with the estranged partner, a difficult situation would be eased. The primary difficulty in blended families is that what the adults concerned want or need is not the same and indeed is often at odds with what the children want and need. Adults may feel the need to move on, to have complete separation from what went before. A new partner, trying to come to terms with the fact that someone else has been in their new partner's life (and heart, and bed!) before them, may demand that everyone pretend the past never happened, or that it was some sort of horrible mistake. When Virginia married Jack, he moved in to live with her and her son in the house she had shared with her ex-husband. She had photographs of the boy and his father as well as all of them as a family dotted around the house, stuck on pinboards as well as in frames on the walls and on tables and windowsills. She gradually added pictures of Jack and of them as a family to these but Jack became increasingly upset about the pictures of her first husband. He eventually demanded she throw them out. When she said this would mean throwing away ten years of her life and memories of all the things she had seen and done, he said she could keep them – as long as she cut out all the images of her ex-husband. Virginia talked to a counsellor and asked for help in making Jack feel better about her past but he made only one visit, saying that their only problem was her obstinacy. When the counsellor asked Jack to explain his feeling about the photographs, his response was that anyone would object to having another man shoved down his throat and he wasn't going to put up with it much longer. The counsellor felt that Jack had his own reasons for feeling vulnerable as a 'seconder' but he was so anxious and angry that he couldn't even begin, at that time, to explore these feelings and the memories that may well have been behind them. Jack refused to return for a second session and Virginia did not come back either.

> Money and children
> are the most frequent reasons
> for arguments in second marriages.

The need to wipe out all reminders that the person you love may have loved someone else is so strong and universal that there are even companies that now offer to use new technology to digitalise images in photographs (and, soon, perhaps in videos) to cut out old partners with more finesse than simply using scissors. But trying to forget or denying the fact that a former partner was a part of your life is to deny a part of yourself and this is hardly healthy. It is even less possible for children and their refusal to let this happen or their reaction when you insist will affect you. Both parents are an integral part of the child and denying their existence or their role as a parent is like trying to cut the child in half and throw away the bit you don't want. Sorting out how you feel about your children and how you are going to manage the complex dynamics of a second relationship with children is vital. It may be tempting to drift into some sort of arrangement, and to let it happen by itself. You would be far better off taking action and taking control of the situation, and the sooner the better. Second marriages are one and a half to twice as likely to end in divorce as first marriages, and not resolving the problems that arise from the presence of children of another partnership have probably a lot to do with that fact. Children are reported to be the second most frequent subject fuelling a row in re-marriages. The most frequent is money – and that may well relate to stepchildren as well.

In practical terms this means that you will be far better off talking than suffering in silence. Whether you are the full-time or part-time natural parent, with or without a new partner, with or without new children through a blended family, you need to establish an open line of communication with every adult or child involved in the new arrangement. Everyone in this pattern has an effect on everyone else and there are no actions that can be taken in isolation. Hit out at one person with whom you are angry or for whom you have no affection and you can guarantee that you will also be harming the people you do care about and yourself. If only to protect the ones you do love, and if only out of self-preservation, communication and negotiation are strongly recommended.

4
STEP-FAMILY RELATIONSHIPS

Partners embarking on a second family often wish they could find an easy explanation for the complex relationships created when two people who have been partnered before get together. Part of the isolation and guilt that can be felt by many people in blended families is caused by the need to pigeon-hole people and situations: people need a status and that status needs a title. Think about the way you might introduce people you know to each other. You would very rarely only use personal names. You usually add a quick description or explanation: 'George, meet Mary. Mary works with me and George is my second cousin'. But the relationships in blended families are often vague and complicated and not only does this cause difficulties in talking about them; it also causes difficulties in thinking about and dealing with them. If a man and woman marry and his or her child live permanently with them, they might say one of them is a step-parent, the child is a step-child and they all form a step-family. But for many people it is not quite so straightforward. Children may come to stay for short periods – weekends and holidays – and the child and the adult with whom they live most of the time may bitterly resent the new partner, and even the part-time parent, taking on a 'parental' status with them. A divorced parent may, having once been bitten, decide not to get married again, even if they enter into a new and permanent relationship. Everyone involved may then find it difficult to work out what their status is in such a family.

The fact that the link between many members in a new extended family lacks a title in this society does not mean that it has no validity. I've been living with my husband Vic for 23 years. We were friends for a year before that, so I've known his son Alex for 24 years, since he was six. This is what I wrote about my feelings about our relationship:

As far as I'm concerned, he is a son to me. After Vic, I've made him my next of kin and if, God forbid, anything should happen to Vic, my relationship with Alex would remain. We may not be linked by blood or marriage, but we are linked. This is very hard for other people to recognise and sometimes I even feel the need to apologise for it or explain it to people. For a long time I didn't tell Alex himself how I felt because I really wasn't sure how he felt about it. It's as if I was trying to be possessive about him just having these

---

Name games

The words we use to describe second families in which there are children often set the tone for how we feel about them. Step-families come up all the time in literature and history but they are usually depicted in an unflattering light. When we say 'step-family' or 'step-parent', feelings of jealousy or rejection tend to spring to mind, whether or not we've experienced such a relationship. For this reason, professionals, such as counsellors, are now turning to the terms *re-formed, re-constituted, re-structured* or *blended* families. They also describe the rather confused network of formal and informal relationships as *new extended families*. The extended family describes all the relationships around the nuclear family of mother, father and their children – that is, grandparents, aunts, uncles, cousins, brothers, sisters, nieces and nephews. A new extended family would include new partners and their relatives, old partners and their relatives (and probably the cats, dogs and hamsters that make up those various homes, too!).

feelings when I had absolutely no right to be like that. I was really rather nervous that he or anyone else was going to turn round to me and say, 'Who the hell do you think you are? You've got no call on him at all'.

WHAT MAKES A 'REAL' STEP-FAMILY?

> Whether you see them daily or never,
> children from a first relationship will have
> a profound effect on a second relationship.

Step relationships can be intricate, confusing and complex. There is an enormous range of relationships to be found in reconstituted families, all of which give rise to a form of significant contact. This contact can be daily, because the child lives with you, or not at all because you or your partner are having difficulties in maintaining contact with children who live full-time with another parent. Whatever the level of actual contact, it is meaningful if it affects you in any way. It is equally notable if you are married to your partner, living with them without having gone through a ceremony, or seeing them on a regular basis. And whether you are one of the parents or a non-related adult, you are likely to be affected by the many and complex circumstances that surround being in a relationship of this sort. All the following people are in new extended or reconstituted families, although some of them have found that they have been denied status by others and are not considered to be members of a real step-family.

Steve and Sue have been married four years. She has two children by her first marriage, who both live with them but stay alternate weekends with their father and his second wife. Steve has three children. The eldest is at university, has no contact with his mother and occasionally stays with them. The other two live with their mother and have no contact with Steve.

Denise and Maureen have lived together for seven years. Maureen's 11-year-old son lives with his father, who successfully fought for custody when Maureen left him and they divorced. He now refuses Maureen all contact with the boy, having said that he might reconsider if Denise, who has never met her partner's son, were out of the picture.

Patti and Tyrone live together and are planning to get married. His two sons by a former marriage stay with them one night a week and he sees them every weekend, either for a day or staying overnight.

Janet and Robbie are in their fifties, have known each other for 30 years and married after her first husband and his first wife died. Robbie has three adult children and the eldest, a daughter, has two children. Janet sends them birthday cards and presents and at Christmas gives them gifts. Their mother either throws these away or makes a point of telling her children they are not what they want. Janet would like the children to call her Granny but she feels unable to suggest it. Robbie's family call her the Witch behind her back.

Elsa and Nelson live with her daughter from her first marriage, his son from his first marriage and a child of their own. Nelson's daughter lives with his first wife and is supposed to see him on alternate weekends. Three out of four times his first wife will cancel at the last moment or he will arrive to find the girl out or no one at home.

Alec lives with his mother and her new partner and their children, his two half-brothers. His father has also remarried and has a new baby, so he also has a half-sister, whom he saw when she was very young but has not seen for some time, as his father's new wife does not like him and his father has stopped seeing him. Alec doesn't get on with his younger half-brothers, nor his stepfather's two daughters, who visit every weekend.

_____ PART-TIME PARENTING _____

Your relationship may come under a far greater strain if children stay with you on a part-time rather than a full-time basis. You may have more time on your own as the children take up less time, but there is often little control over when, where and how they are seen. Deirdre and James have been together for 18 years. His son Paul, who lived with James's first wife Laura, visited at fairly frequent, but irregular, intervals.

Laura used to ring up and say, 'Paul really needs to see his father and would like to come for the weekend'. It may have been totally inconvenient for us and mean we had to cancel plans we had, but we really had no choice. Then he would arrive and be in a really foul mood, sulking all weekend. Of course we would then be fed up that we'd had our weekend spoiled on his insistence and he hadn't enjoyed it and I'd be angry at James for not being able to say no. It took us an awfully long time to realise that what was really going on was that Laura had needed a break, possibly because she had a boyfriend she wanted to spend a romantic weekend with, and it was her choice, not Paul's, that he come down. He, of course, had had his own plans for seeing friends or just mucking around at home, and that had been totally thrown out of kilter. It wasn't her fault, because I can see the difficulties she was living with, but it really was hell on wheels for all of us, and it did lead to bitter arguments sometimes.

Control can be an issue in other ways with part-time parenting. To-ing and fro-ing between families and homes is probably the worst aspect for everyone in a new extended family – the children, the full-time and the part-time parent and the step-parent. Having said that, if the parent who has left ceases to have any sort of contact with or access to their children, this does not make the situation any easier. Just because children are not there in the flesh, does not mean that they cease to have an involvement or a significance in their parents' lives. Indeed, the less contact there is, the more the disruption. When they no longer see the missing children, parents are likely to feel guilty for abandoning them. Children, in turn, feel unloved and therefore unworthy of love. They will probably find it difficult to discuss this with a remaining parent or with anyone else, but may show their unhappiness in disruptive or self-destructive ways. Having to with deal with guilt at not being in touch with the deserted child will have dramatic and destructive effects on your own relationship.

Flexible access, where arrangements are made as they arise rather than having a 'one weekend in every two' or 'third Thursday in the month, between the hours of 5.15 and 6.43' may be seen by many people as being ideal. It can be far better for parents and children to be adaptable and spontaneous. However, managing a constantly altering arrangement can be difficult for the adults concerned. Either parent may see it as being very one-way. What a visiting parent sees as flexible may be regarded by the full-time parent as something that puts them at the beck and call of a part-timer who calls all the shots. Alternatively, the part-time parent may feel helpless and unable to object or miss the chance to see the child whenever the full-time parent says so. Weekend access for fathers is also an unfair anomaly in a day and age when women work full-time, too. It might have been convenient for women to have the children during the week and for them to go to the father at the weekend in the days when men worked and women did not. This would allow men to have quality time while still earning the money for both families, while the mother would see her children each weekday before and after school – and perhaps at lunchtime.

But now that women work too, it means that women can end up with all the work and none of the play.

Any time you have contact with authority or institutions as a second family with children, you may be reminded that society as a whole feels your situation is unusual. Filling in forms that ask for details of family and offspring can be extremely difficult . This is what I wrote about the difficulty in fitting my own family situation into society's pigeonholes.

The main problem has always been with forms, which drive me to distraction. It was bad enough that, in the first 10 years or so of our relationship, most institutions and government or financial bodies refused to accept the validity of unmarried relationships. We weren't married at the time, and this was before forms had sections saying partner or living together as well as single, married or separated. It simply was not accepted then. But the worst thing was that Alex just simply didn't exist as far as they were concerned. You were asked about dependants, but since he didn't live with us he didn't count. Vic didn't contribute regular maintenance for him, having given Jenny a settlement when they split up by simply giving her the proceeds of the sale of their house and all the contents. When Alex stayed with us we would buy clothes and that sort of thing when Jenny asked. But we were making a contribution, and at times it was a strain. So the fact that there was no space on any form to fill in 'sort of semi-dependent who certainly costs us something' irritated the hell out of me. He's a next of kin to us both after each other, but again that doesn't count, does it?

FAMILY SYSTEMS

Acquiring a new step-father or step-mother can mean a lot of changes for both the adults and the children involved. There may be a change of status. The adult is no longer a single person or a widow or a widower, but a partner or spouse, and perhaps out of the blue a parent. It can be difficult coming to terms with this, not just because of the abruptness of the change but because both you and other people may not realise how it affects you. One reason it may have such an impact is that the pattern of relationships in your family changes when new people and new partnerships come on the scene, but you may not have recognised why and how. One way of understanding what is going on is to explore these patterns.

When you marry for the first time, you rightly think of yourself and your partner as the central players on your stage. You form a *system* of two. Your relatives, friends, community and society at large fit in around this small unit, which you gradually enlarge as you and your partner have your own children, forming a system of three, four and so on. Within your small unit you may well have alliances and favourites, with mum and daughter or daughter and dad backing each other up against the others. Some families have difficulties from day one because the unit of partner and partner has a problem in establishing itself. Maybe someone who shouldn't interfere, such as a parent or a friend, is too close and spoils any chance of the couple creating a strong, intimate bond. With a second family, there are trespassers involved who threaten the boundaries from the start – your children, your ex-partner/s and their family. Not only may there be hostility directed towards one particular person by other members of this new extended family, but the particular attitudes and beliefs about second families and step-families of all those around you will affect your chances of success.

STEPPING OVER THE LINE

Most problems in blended families come about because of *inappropriate behaviour*. That is, because certain members of that family are doing something that they may need to do but that feels wrong to someone else. For instance, when Rupert married

Audrey, he was more than happy to have her daughter as their bridesmaid. He said

I was amused as this little 10-year-old strutted around as if it were her big day, in her dress and carrying a flower basket, for all the world acting like Queen of the May. In fact, now I come to think of it, she was of course acting like the bride. It was less funny when she threw a tantrum because we were going away for our honeymoon without her and even less of a laugh when we came back. She just wouldn't leave us alone. She clings to her mother, she's always pushing in between us and won't give us any privacy. She actually tells me I should go home, because as far as she's concerned, where she and her mother live is not my home.

Similarly, when Robbie and Janet married, Robbie realised his eldest daughter felt Janet was being interfering and arrogant to expect to be granny to her two children.

She feels Janet is trying to win them over and act as if they were hers, and as far as she's concerned they're not and never will be. I think she resents Janet, as she sees it, trying to take her mother's place.

What feels wrong is that these people seem to be behaving in ways that don't fit the situation – a child who is acting like a rival or a fractious baby, an adult who is taking on a place you don't feel is theirs. Drawing a line picture allows you to see where everyone in your family feels they belong. Once you start to see that, you may be able to see why they are acting in this way and why certain people may find this upsetting. Audrey's daughter, for instance, felt Rupert was a rival, since she and her mother had lived alone together for four years and she was upset and angry at being pushed away. When she drew a diagram, she drew a line around herself and her mother, firmly shutting Rupert out. Robbie's daughter felt Janet was trying to win her father away from their family and they wanted the boundary to remain strongly in place, shutting her out. Drawing the line allows you to see what the problem is and is the first step in solving matters!

=====================*Task*=====================

Draw a line around it

Every group of people forms a unit, and around each unit there is a boundary, an invisible line that lets you know who is 'in' and who is 'out'. Sometimes that boundary is very reassuring. If you are on the inside, it serves to let you know you belong and are safe and sound within. Sometimes it can be frightening, if you feel unable to break out and make new contacts. If you are on the outside, it can be very intimidating as the boundary may not let you get near to people to whom you might like to be close. In a healthy family, boundaries are clear but can be flexible. That is, friends and new relatives are let in and as children grow up they are encouraged and supported to leave the family circle and set up their own system with a partner. We all live with these invisible lines without being consciously aware of them or the way they influence our actions and feelings.

Actually drawing a diagram to show your boundaries can help you to understand and see how and why you and your family may be experiencing difficulties in a blended family. Drawing boundaries may let you see, on paper, the patterns that are causing problems. Look at this family:

John and Jane married three years ago. When they tried this exercise, at first both of them drew a boundary that simply enclosed themselves.

Jane was previously married to Bob, and their children Tom and Sally live with her and John. When she and John looked at the problems they were having, she said that sometimes it felt as if the boundary should be drawn around herself and the children.

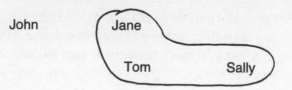

Jane admits that Tom and Sally would probably draw it around her, themselves and Bob.

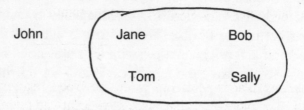

John's son Simon lives with his mother Jill. He says that as well as a line around Jane and himself, he would draw a separate one around Simon and himself.

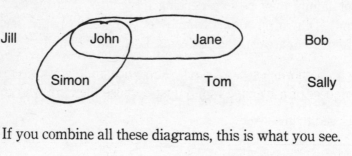

If you combine all these diagrams, this is what you see.

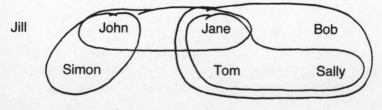

It's easy to see how John may feel left out by the family with whom he lives, and how Jane, Tom and Sally might think his attention is directed outside their home. As far as this family is concerned, Jill is outside everything, giving her good reason to feel angry and abandoned and in need of sabotaging John's relationship or just shaking the apple tree to get some attention for her and her son. Jane has every reason to feel torn and harried, as she is the centre of several circles, being pulled in so many different directions.

Do this exercise for yourself and your family.

Our society places enormous value on blood relationships and sees them as more desirable, more significant and more important than any other kind of tie between adult and child. This can make forming a happy bond between an adult and a non-related child difficult, both because of our own feelings and because of the lack of support and understanding from other people. It also means that a couple who are trying to develop and strengthen their own relationship while there are children who come from a previous relationship are going to find it hard. The result is often an enormous lack of self-confidence and even esteem in all members of a blended family just because they are who they are.

> Blood ties are often seen to be
> more desirable,
> more significant,
> more important
> than any other kind of tie between adult and child.

SCAPEGOATS

Children often become the prime targets or the dumping grounds for anger and grief in the breakdown of a relationship, and when a new one is made, simply because they are there. Sometimes, when a couple in a new relationship are having difficulties, instead of facing up to them they may focus their anger or fears on the children and insist that it is they who are the problem. Most of us will fall into the trap of making one person a scapegoat for uncomfortable feelings when we don't want to have to face up to them. This happened in Penny and Eric's marriage and they asked for help five years after getting married. Living with them are his son from his first marriage, her daughter from her first marriage, and their own child. Penny was convinced that there was one reason and one reason only for their problems:

It's the boy that's the problem. We'd have a perfectly happy marriage but for him. He causes arguments all the time and there's a constant bad atmosphere, for no reason.

Children may have many reasons for resenting a new adult in their lives. One can be because of the way a parent might have relied on them before the new adult came along. In many cases there will be some, or even a considerable, amount of time in between the ending of the original couple relationship and the formation of a new family. Even if a partnership is dissolved and a new one made almost immediately, if the old partner had been absent a lot of the time, the child may have been called upon to take their place. If the parent has leaned heavily on a child, needing emotional support or practical help, the child may find it hard to give up their place in the family to a new partner. They may be under pressure from everyone else to be happy at belonging once again to what society considers to be a 'proper' family, but feel that their new positions inside this family are as much or more of a loss than a gain. Children used to being leaned on or respected as equal partners may suddenly find themselves thrust back into dependency or into the background. This was the problem for Eric's son who had been eight when his mother had died. Eric and he had lived together for three years before Penny came on the scene and he had become a mature, responsible boy with a very close link with his father. Neither Eric nor Penny had realised how much the lad had resented no longer having his father's special attention or being expected to help in the day-to-day running of their home, such as cooking meals and laying the fire. Penny had assumed an 11-year-old was far too young, not interested in, or not able to do such things and, keen as she was to show Eric she could look after them all, she had pushed the boy aside. Their counsellor helped them to see that the boy might have concerns of his own rather than just being the concern. They were also helped to see the way Eric, without realising it, had not helped. When a parent has a strong bond with a child, it can be as hard to let go for the adult as it is for the child. Sometimes, especially when there are tensions in the couple relationship, it can be easier to fall back on the 'unconditional' love and loyalty a child offers than to have to work to establish or re-establish the adult bond. And Penny was blaming the boy rather than looking at how her own desire to do her best was making her feel inadequate. Once Penny and Eric realised and talked over what had really been happening, they found their own relationship improved.

FURTHER CHILDREN

Obviously when a couple who both already have children come together, the scenario can be like a Chinese puzzle – boxes within boxes. Both partners will be in the double situation of being a parent coping with their former partner and children, and having a new partner and being a step-parent. The children will not only have to deal with the separation of their parents and coming to terms with the new adult, but also with step-siblings. This can be confusing and may have profound effects on the couple's relationship. His children may hate most of hers, hers may despise most of his but her eldest and his youngest may strike a truce and declare war on everyone. The shifting alliances and possible hostilities blossoming, fading and flaring up again within the family will probably make the United Nations on a bad day look like a tea party! Children born to the new partnership may also introduce a new balance that may either be helpful or destructive. Whatever, while trying to keep pace with a multitude of demands, the couple's own romance can get totally lost.

When Farooq married Meena, both of them had children from their first marriages.

My two girls fought like cat and dog with Meena's son and daughter and we spent so much time keeping them apart that our own relationship was suffering. Then we told them a baby was on the way and the change was astounding. They were all so angry they had something to agree about! My father told me a saying: 'The enemy of my enemy is my friend', and they certainly thought it was true! When the baby was born, though, the three girls were totally won over and the boy came round too when he saw how many of his sisters' friends were coming round to see the child. They get on fine, now, and so do we.

Children have no power to prevent the break-up of their original family and the establishment of a new one. It seems to be one-way traffic for them. You don't give them any choices – the old family is splitting up and the new one is being established whether they like it or not. They have to compromise, by accepting the presence in their living space of people they haven't chosen. Their feelings of powerlessness can be overwhelming and they may hit back in the only way they can, by trying to have some effect on your relationship with arguments and sulks. It does help, of course, if you are prepared to talk over and explain your decisions and to ask for and accept some measure of feedback from the children. The balance is a delicate one, though. Children's priorities are different from those of adults. If you look at what you are trying to achieve simply in terms of 'asking permission' from your children, you may find yourself in a very unhappy situation. They may say 'no', not necessarily because they disagree with what you are doing but just because it gives them back that feeling of being in control. You need to walk the fine line between patronising children and imposing your own choices on them under the guise of 'what is best for them', and listening to them and giving in to something that is not in their long-term interests. By all means use your experience to know when to apply your authority to a choice, but do listen to and take on board their ideas as well. Giving them some sort of power over their lives – even if it is only the right to choose the family's supper menu one night a week – can help.

If a process of explanation and discussion is to take place with the children, make sure all of them are involved, not only the oldest ones or those who see you for the majority of the time. Darren and Joyce were open with Joyce's son Eddo and their son Earl, but left Darren's daughter Sassy out of discussions because she only saw them every other weekend.

She resented Earl, even though he was her half brother and she and Eddo – well, we couldn't leave them in a room together or there'd be murder done.

Their counsellor suggested holding a family discussion and including Sassy to let her have her say. At first, Joyce and Darren were sceptical about this.

We'd thought it wasn't right because she wasn't there all that often but we finally came round to agreeing that that's the problem; she's not there all that often and she knows it!

Sassy felt left out and rejected, not just because she had less time with her father than her half- and step-brothers, but because they had a say in family decisions and she 'wasn't family'. Once she was included, the atmosphere changed dramatically and quickly. Joyce and Darren made a point of inviting her to take more of a part in their family life and soon noticed a difference, to the children and to their own relationship.

It may be impossible to ensure that everyone in your family gets what they want and need. Perhaps if you can at least start off with the conviction that the emotional growth and stability of every member of your family is equally important, you may get nearest to achieving the best possible compromise. You want neither martyrs nor scapegoats; it doesn't help if you sacrifice your own needs and interests in order to make someone else happy, nor does it help if you blame one person for all the problems and act as if they would disappear overnight if this person went away.

LOOK AFTER YOUR OWN RELATIONSHIP

The stronger or the more secure the relationship between the new partners, the greater the benefit to the whole new extended family. If you have unfinished business with an old partner, it may be tempting to work out your anger and grief at the break-up of your relationship by attacking any weakness you see in the new one. 'All's fair in love and war', we say, and if the result is not to win back the missing partner, at least we may feel satisfied with a measure of revenge. The difficulty, of course, may be that it is the children who suffer most in such a battle. You may even feel justified in causing them pain if you believe that such a fight will win you back your partner. But if that is not the end result, everyone may have suffered needlessly. The stability of the new relationship is just as much in your interests as in your ex-partner's, and is certainly in your children's interests. It may seem very odd for someone to be making a case for the ex-partner to support a new relationship, but the fact is that for your own and your children's continuing happiness, this may be your best option.

SECOND CHANCE

One big advantage of second families is that they offer a second chance to their members to be a caring and sharing part of such a group, to find a new role or to renegotiate their role in the family. Men who might feel they failed as fathers the first time around may have another try, and women who missed out on balancing the couple relationship against the maternal one can divide their attentions differently on a second attempt.

Jon, for instance, felt he had missed out as a father. He and his first wife married young and, looking back, he realised he had spent more time with friends and at work than he should have done. Jon's daughter became anorexic in her teenage years, about the time that Jon and his first wife split up, and Jon felt guilty that he had been of little help to her. Anorexia, as Jon was later to learn, is often found in young women who have fathers whom they adore but who are emotionally or actually unavailable to them. When he remarried a woman 15 years younger than himself, Jon's daughter soon recognised that the new wife was anorexic too. Without realising it, her condition had been one of the things that attracted him because Jon now had the chance to help her, as he had not been able to help his daughter. Jon and his daughter were able to develop a new and loving relationship as together they helped his new wife to overcome her own illness. Jon was able to offer both women his support and love, and was thus able to feel better about himself.

> Relationships break up for many reasons
> and it's never one person's fault.

Relationships break up for many and varied reasons, but few break-ups are simply one person's fault. In fact, notions of fault and blame are often a waste of time and energy. What is important is a shared responsibility for establishing communication. You are probably determined that this relationship will succeed, and it will be important for both of you to agree that you and your partner will make a real effort to understand yourselves and each other, and to talk to each other as much as possible. If you do have any difficulties, seek help to resolve them at an early stage, rather than leaving it until it is again too late. If you find it hard to make it work, then perhaps you should be having serious, second thoughts about this relationship. If you or your partner cannot work with the fact that children are a part of the deal, perhaps you should walk away. The children can't walk away and, after all, they were there first. But if you do decide to commit yourself to this new relationship, don't set yourself unreasonably high targets. Don't expect to love the children at once and don't feel guilty if you don't or if they don't love you. Parents are not always good, right, loving and caring. They too may find it takes some time to get to know and like, let alone love, their offspring – and even then, not all the time.

LOOK AFTER YOURSELF

One accusation that is likely to fly around in broken or second families with children is that one or other of you is being selfish. And yet, being selfish is actually another way of being generous – generous to yourself. Indeed, you really aren't much use to anyone else if you are not cared for as well. So, whether you are the full-time or part-time parent, on your own or with a new partner, or whether you are the new partner in a blended family, for your own and everyone else's sake, you should take some time and effort to pay attention to your own needs.

Don't lose touch with friends, and make a point of still doing sports or other activities that gave you pleasure in the past. In fact, if you haven't got a life outside your immediate family, it would be a good idea to build one up. We all need the occasional opportunity to spend time and exchange gossip and ideas with our mates. The possible stresses and strains of a blended family may make this all the more necessary and desirable. Women in a blended family may also find it particularly useful, if possible, to have a part-time or a full-time job. Many stepmothers do not work only because they are trying to recreate an image of what they see as a 'good, natural family'. In fact, both the adults and the children may benefit more from what is in reality the more common and therefore more 'natural' situation of the working mother. Having a job will also give a woman in a blended family much needed outside support. The money may be a considerable help and so will the chance to feel that she has a status and a role other than just in the family.

PART THREE
THE ADULT VIEW

5

INNER FEELINGS

To understand the problems affecting a blended family, and to find some solutions to them, you need to explore what you and everyone else thinks is occurring, why you might think that and how you feel about it. In this chapter, we will explore the underlying feelings and points of view that make you behave the way you do in a second relationship. It's worth spending the time to work out the whys and wherefores of your feelings and how these make you behave. Arguments and difficulties in families can often be traced to a reaction to something from your past. Whether you realise it or not, events and people in the 'here and now' often trigger memories from long ago, and this can set off reactions that can seem excessive, destructive and inexplicable. These may be from the more recent past, that is the ending of your first relationship, or as far back as your own childhood.

Being part of a second family can be painful and confusing at first, whether you're an adult or a child, whether you make the decision that brings that family into being or are swept along in someone else's wake. I've seen the situation as an agony aunt, a counsellor and as a second family member myself, and I know how awkward it can be. It doesn't have to be as difficult or as destructive as some of us anticipate. There can be positive aspects to being a second-time couple, as there are to acquiring the extended network of a second family. Being part of a second family can bring benefits not found the first time round.

> The beginning of a second family can be painful and
> confusing, but it doesn't have to go on that way.

If you and your partner are trying to adjust to being a second-time couple, and there are children involved, a key fact when trying to understand the complexities of blended families is that what is good for you may not necessarily be good for them and vice versa. What adults want and need for their own well-being and satisfaction may be different, if not entirely at odds, with what might be best for their children. Similarly, adults and children may have entirely differing interpretations of what is going on in the family when you break up and when you meet someone new.

Members of blended families often find themselves reacting violently and passionately to their new step-relatives. It may be hard to recognise that what they are all experiencing is common to most second families, which means it is the situation that is the problem rather than the people themselves. It can be even more difficult to realise that our own responses may be at the root of the trouble rather than any one else's character or actions. None of this is anybody's fault, but if you can understand what you are feeling and why, you may be much closer to dealing with the specific problems, explaining yourself to others and perhaps making adjustments yourself or helping others to do so too. If there are children involved it would also be of enormous benefit if you could understand how they may be feeling, and we will be dealing with that in another chapter.

The beginning of a restructured family, just like the beginning of a first relationship, may seem to the adults involved to be the cue to look to the future. You may not want to think about any part of the past and only wish to consider the future. All restructured families have one thing in common that sets them apart from first-time relationships. This is that they begin in the aftermath of one or more previous relationships. You may like to think you can start afresh, with a totally clean sheet. A new relationship may be seen as a way of putting sadness behind you or of conquering any doubts about your worth and attractiveness. Starting again from scratch may not be possible, however. If there are children involved, a clean break is far harder. Divided loyalties will give rise to feelings of jealousy and insecurity. Children keep alive ties to ex-spouses that you may prefer to sever and this will affect how you and your partner form your new blended family. The ending of the previous relationship frequently leaves you struggling with feelings of failure or grief. Trying to sweep feelings under the carpet is only likely to create a rather nasty bump that you keep tripping over. The problem with suppressing feelings, whether hidden from others or from yourself, is that they do have a horrible habit of emerging in unexpected and damaging ways. Unless you understand the power the past has over you, you may be doomed endlessly to repeat the same mistakes.

Suppressed feelings will re-emerge
often in surprising and painful ways.

EMOTIONAL BONDS

It's quite common to retain emotional links with an ex-partner, even though you are planning to divorce or have already done so. It is even common still to have these feelings when you have met, fallen in love with and married, or set up home with, someone new. The ending of relationships is a complicated process and not simply because one partner falls in love with someone else, or realises they no longer love the person they are with. If you are going to understand how 'leftover' feelings from an earlier relationship may affect a new one, you need to understand how relationships tend to come apart. Each relationship that ends breaks up in its own individual way, but the steps to a breakdown are broadly similar in every case. Progressing from the first to the final stage is just like any journey. That is, individual people may take one or two steps and then return to the beginning, or take a few steps and then stay at that point, or complete the whole process in one rush.

The first stage is a very common one and not particularly worrying in itself. This is when one or both partners realise that the marriage, and their partner, does not satisfy their every need. In fact, it's unrealistic to expect them to do so and most mature, happy couples do recognise this and adapt accordingly. The problems arise if you feel unhappy or guilty at feeling this way and try to avoid having to face it, pretending to yourself that your worries don't exist or hope that by ignoring them they will simply fade. In many relationships, one of the partners fills time and distracts him or herself at this point by taking on a new job, a new interest or an educational class. What starts as a way of filling time may soon become a means of developing an identity outside the couple. Having your own identity can be a very healthy development in a relationship, but it can also be part of the journey from couple to separation if it's done with resentment or anger.

Someone at this stage may not have separation in mind and may well invite the other partner to join in the new interest. If the partner responds, or at least if they take some notice and are supportive, the relationship will be renewed. But if this fails, and particularly if the interest makes the person feel better than they do in the relationship, then a form of separation has already taken place and the couple begin to live in separate worlds. They may start to have open rows, one of them may make complaints about the other in front of friends or relatives and spend more time away from home. If this doesn't work and their partner still remains unaware or refuses to notice that something is really wrong, the unhappy member of the couple may find another person outside the relationship to talk to and confide in. This third party could be a member of the clergy, a child, an old school friend, a divorce lawyer – or a lover. But, whoever this person is, by this time, the relationship is well on the way to being at an end. The other partner may still believe all is well or that difficulties are only temporary or unimportant. The person leaving may already have recognised and even fully mourned the death of the relationship, while their partner is still totally committed to it and will react with total disbelief and bewilderment to the split.

> Some people remain 'psychologically married' even though their relationship may be long over.

Some people never truly recognise or admit that a relationship is over and they may remain 'psychologically married' for ever, even though legally divorced, in a new relationship or remarried. If the separation is not mutual and total then there will always be a degree of emotional hangover in this way. There is no formal 'funeral' at the end of a relationship – no body, no coffin and therefore in many cases, no admission of a death at all. Since we are taught in this society that it is important to be a couple, we usually enter into relationships expecting them to last, so it is obviously hard to let go without a struggle. Women often take longer to separate than men, as they can be nervous of going it alone. And, curiously, either sex can experience all these difficulties even if they are the ones choosing to leave the relationship. Just because you were the person who left or opted for divorce, that does not mean that you were the one who emotionally separated. Indeed, it is quite common for our minds and our bodies to be going in different directions.

We often need to sort out how we feel about the relationship that has failed, whether this is our own or our partner's, before we can happily make and sustain a new one. Leftover business can cast a shadow over relationships that come after. When we continue to feel angry and bitter, and continue to row with past partners, we maintain a connection and refuse to let go. New partners often let themselves be drawn, or even throw themselves, into arguments between exes, in the hope and belief that they can cut the tie. But far from putting an end to the issue, joining in only prolongs it.

Instead of finishing the argument, we often attempt to break off from the past by denying it. It is a very human reaction to look at a relationship that has failed and want to wipe it completely from the record. New partners want to take over and replace the old one, old partners want to forget the other person was ever there. This is hard enough when you are an individual, because doing this successfully means removing a part of yourself. You are, after all, the sum of everything in your past. But it presents particular difficulties when there are children left over from the relationship. Denying that you ever, really, truly loved your old partner means denying their role with the children, too. Whether you demand this of yourself or of your new partner, the likelihood is that it will cause conflict and pain for all of you. Step-parents and natural parents who constantly criticise children, picking on habits or behaviour they find annoying, are often doing so because they feel threatened by reminders of the other parent. It really isn't the child that upsets you so much as what they represent and what they remind you of. It may be very tempting to want to cast a fresh relationship in the best possible light by looking at the old in the worst possible light, but trying to insist that one was 'all bad' to make the other seem 'all good' is self-defeating. You may need to own up to and accept mixed feelings about past and present relationships – that you might harbour lingering good feelings about your first as well as have bad ones about the second – before you can go on to be happy.

LOOKING BACK

To understand why you may be having problems, you may need to go even further back than the ending of your last relationship. Your own experiences in your family of origin may be where your difficulties started. What happened to you in your childhood acts as a script for the rest of your life. When you are trying to understand what is happening in a second family that is experiencing difficulties, it often helps to recall what it was it like in your family as you grew up.

! ——————————— *Task* ———————————

Hitting the Bull's Eye – drawing a relationship map

This is a way of understanding the patterns in your life. It's an exercise that can give you some surprising insights which can be exciting but also may be upsetting. So take care and try to do this exercise in a supportive situation with the opportunity to talk it over afterwards with family or friends. You can do it with your partner, agreeing to take turns (spin a coin for who goes first), to listen and be sympathetic, or you can do it on your own.

Get a large sheet of paper and some pens and draw a series of circles, one inside the other – like a target or Bull's Eye. Cast your mind back to your childhood and pick an age – 10, 13, 8, whatever. The age that pops into your mind is likely to be the one you will learn something by recalling.

Remember yourself at that age and put yourself, at that age, in the centre of your circles. You can either do this by drawing in a dot labelled with your name or a little stick diagram. Then, think of all the people you had a relationship with at that time – your parents, brothers and sisters, grandparents, aunts and uncles, friends and anyone connected with you in some way. You can include 'missing' people such as parents who live apart, too. Put all of them on your map with the ones to whom you felt closest emotionally, nearest to you. For instance, if you got on with your Mum, you might put her in the centre with you or in the next circle. If you had a distant relationship, you would put her way out on the edge. Resist putting people where you think they should have been or would like them to have been. The point is to show yourself the picture as it really felt.

When you have placed all your family, look at how you have arranged them. The way you have laid them out says a lot about how you feel. Did you find it hard to place some people? Who was close to you? Who did you see as closer or farther away than you expected? Who was closer or farther away than you might have liked? Was there anyone there you didn't want at all, or is there anyone not on the map you might have liked to be there? Are you surprised at where you have put some of your contacts?

If you had the power to make one change in this pattern, what would it have been? Why? Finally, think about what you might learn from the pattern you made. Is there any likeness to the pattern you see in your childhood and what is going on now?

Carrie and Tom asked for help from a counsellor because their marriage, her first and his second, was in trouble. Tom had two sons, aged seven and 10, from his previous relationship, who would stay with them every weekend. Carrie found herself unable to accept the two boys, who even she admitted were pleasant and accepting of her. But she felt they were noisy and selfish and monopolised Tom's attention and that he ignored her when they were around. In spite of his insistence that he did all he could to be even-handed, Carrie felt he preferred them to her and was at the point of issuing an ultimatum – if he continued to keep contact at the present level she would leave. She admitted that she hoped he would choose her above his children, but feared he would not. Carrie and Tom did a relationship map with their counsellor to look at their family backgrounds.

When Carrie did her map, she chose to do it for her family when she had been 11 years old. She put her father, who she said she adored but who had very little time for her, several circles away from herself. Her younger brothers, who had been seven and 10 when she had been 11, she placed one circle nearer to her, but next to their father. She put her mother on the last circle on the farthest side of her father.

When she was asked if she could have made any change, Carrie at first said she wanted to leave her brothers where they were but bring her father into the centre with herself. When she looked at the pattern she had made, Carrie suddenly realised that how she felt at that moment about Tom and his children was exactly the way she had felt as an 11-year-old with her father and brothers. Here she was again, feeling left out and abandoned because a seven-year-old and a 10-year-old boy were her rivals for the love and attention of the most important man in her life, who she thought ignored her for them. Once she realised that, she understood that in some ways she could never get what see wanted. Challenging Tom to choose her first wouldn't work, because it wasn't Tom she wanted to make that choice but her father and the time for that was long past. But because she now saw that much of her unhappiness was from leftover feelings from the past, Carrie was able to separate those from her anxieties about the present. She was able to value herself, and her mother, more and see that Tom loved and wanted her just as much as he loved his children.

LOVE AT FIRST SIGHT

Whether we realise it or not, we do choose the people we fall in love with and with whom we form relationships. Even 'love at first sight' is the result of some decision-making and less haphazard than we imagine. Partners and people who attract us fulfil a need, or needs, that mostly go unrecognised in our conscious minds. Often, the need is to make right something that might have gone wrong in our childhood. Events and relationships in childhood are vitally important; like having a script written for us, for later life.

If your parents were loving and supportive, were there when you needed them but gave you plenty of encouragement to stand on your own two feet, you are likely to grow up with a script that tells you you're a worthwhile person who deserves to succeed. You will want to repeat that script and will look for a partner who resembles the best in your parents. But when parents are not able to give you the care you need, and are physically or emotionally absent for all or some of your childhood, you may want to rewrite the script. You'll still look for a partner who resembles a parent, but with the story ending on a happier note, with them able to love and care for you and to 'be there' for you. Sadly, since you will be choosing someone like your parent in their inability to fulfil this need, and since you yourself may well have no real idea of how to satisfy the same needs in the other person, you may find yourself repeating the same mistakes your parents made with you. This is why relationships, even between couples who love each other, so often break up. And why you can find second relationships going exactly the same way as first ones. Many of our needs remain unchanged over the years, so new partners may well resemble the old ones, both in appearance and in character and behaviour. They may seem different, and in some ways act differently, but unless you can come to an understanding of what you are really looking

! ═══════════ *Task* ═══════════

Family trees

The classic family tree is usually a way of showing who is related to whom. They can also be used to give you a surprisingly clear picture of how you feel about yourself and your own place in a family and how you feel about other people, too. When you draw a diagram of your family, as well as names, ages and the lines of connection you can add little 'word sketches' of everybody. Family history, and family secrets can emerge and begin to show you the patterns that form your family script. This exercise can be startlingly powerful, so make sure you do it with someone you trust, when you are feeling safe and supported.

Get a large sheet of paper. Use these symbols to draw up your chart:

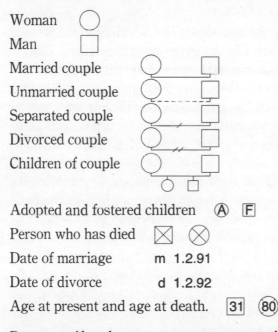

Adopted and fostered children   Ⓐ   𝔽

Person who has died   ⊠   ⊗

Date of marriage   **m** 1.2.91

Date of divorce   **d** 1.2.92

Age at present and age at death.   31   ⑧⓪

Put yourself and your current partner at the centre of the page, and then draw in your own parents, your brothers and sisters (if any), ex-partners and children (if any). While you are filling in all the facts, add impressions and what comes to mind about all these people and about yourself. You could chart the strength of feeling between certain people – who's close, who's distant, who has a stormy relationship. You could put down the labels – joker, carer, followers and leaders. Put down what pops into your mind while you are doing this, without stopping to think whether it is relevant or not, because the things your memory allows to rise to the surface are often the most important. Add your partner's side too, and, if they are doing this exercise with you, add their impressions.

Now look at what you have written. Can you see any patterns or themes that repeat and might have a message for you now?

!

Shari's family tree

Look at this family tree, drawn by Shari. She had several long-term relationships and one marriage that ended in divorce before she met and married Bernie, who had also been married before. They have been married for 12 years and have a strong, happy relationship but it wasn't until she drew her own family tree that Shari understood some interesting things about her choice of partner in Bernie, and his in her.

When we did our family tree, I realised for the first time the amazing resemblance between Bernie, my first husband and my father, not just in the sort of people they were but even in looks. My father divorced my mother when I was one year old, Bernie's father left when he was a baby and he was divorced when his son was one. My first husband and Bernie are also older than me – father figures in a way – and both were men who were distant and difficult to get close to. Bernie has never got on with his mother and his first wife's family were very close and interfering. Then he married me, with no close relatives!

Shari's family tree

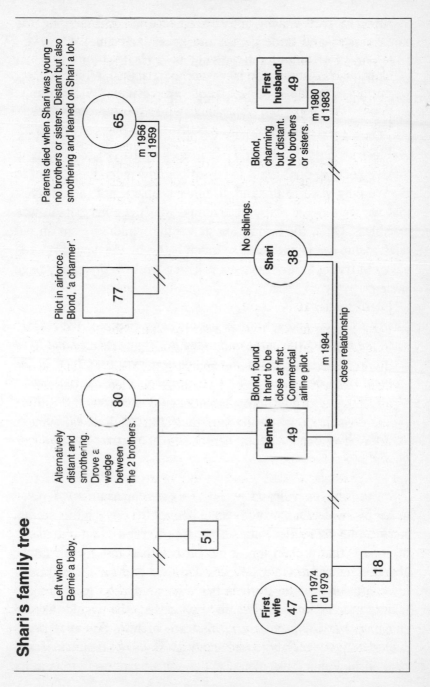

for in your partner, you may in essence go on marrying the same person, and finding dissatisfaction each time. When you tell yourself a second relationship is a clean sheet, that you are turning over a new leaf and that nothing will be the same, you may well be starting off on the worst possible foot.

Once a relationship is over we often want to put it behind us. We feel so hurt, angry and sometimes embarrassed that now they've gone we don't want to remember how much they meant to us. We may want to pretend, to other people if not to ourselves, that we were never really in love and that the other person was worthless. Often the strong insistence that children from an old relationship can be parented so much better by the new partner is a way of trying to rewrite history. Tracy wrote to my agony page saying:

I don't want my ex-husband to see my son any more. We split up when the boy was only three and now I want my new husband to be his father in every way. Although my new man isn't keen at the moment, he'd be so much better for my son than his real father and it only confuses the boy when my ex comes round. If he left us alone I know my husband would take to the boy and love him like his own. How can I stop my ex-husband from interfering in our family?

Tracy sees her ex-husband's wish to see his son as an interference in *her* life, which in a way it is. She blames the boy's father for his son's confusion, rather than seeing it as a result of an unrealistic demand – that a child forget his birth father and a birth father abandon his child. Tracy believes her anxiety is for the child and his confusion but the truth is her own needs and emotions are taking precedence. For her to feel better, she would like to eliminate her old partner and all trace of him. She isn't being deliberately selfish and her behaviour is very common. If she realised how much her own and her son's needs were in conflict and how much doing what is best for her damages her child, she would think again.

> Two adults in a new relationship
> may have very different agendas.

You may, like Tracy, find two adults in a new relationship pulling in very different directions. The one who is bringing children with him or her may try to encourage their new partner to take over the role and position of the missing parent. The one who is taking on someone else's children may not even want to acknowledge these children exist because they are a reminder of a past love. If one of you has children living for most of the time with the ex-partner, the situation can become increasingly complex. As a 'weekend parent' you may attempt to retain the link while progressively being frozen out by whoever has the children full-time. If you find dealing with these children too painful, you may decide to sever those links yourself, trying to pretend the children and/or your ex-partner have no more place in your life, to the pain and confusion of the discarded family who may make increasingly desperate attempts to keep in touch. Adults may often try to keep children out of the new partnership as much as possible. If they don't cut off all contact they may visit their children on their own but avoid bringing children back to their new home. Even if they do have frequent contact, they may keep children and new partners separate and the result may often be a gradual estrangement of parent and child. The excuse for this may be that it prevents the children suffering confusion or unhappiness, but it may often be a means of punishing the ex-partner. Sadly, the main result is to punish the children and to make their attitudes to the step relationship so conflicted that it makes it difficult for them ever to come to terms with the new situation.

_____ NAME GAMES _____

Names and titles within a blended family may be a subject of
concern because of the way they do, or don't, confirm your status
within it. They can also be important because of the way you feel.
Conflict over what children should call their step-parents and how
they should describe each other only serves to underline the fact
that there are no guidelines to help us consider and define the role
of step-parents. Is a new adult 'Dad' or 'Mum', Auntie, Uncle, or
do you want them to call you by your first name? Or is it just
'Hey, you', 'Thingy', or *'her'*? The Children Act recognises the
enormous importance of the biological parent to each child. One
aspect of this is the importance to the child of retaining the name
of the birth father, even when the mother has remarried and
changed her name and even if he is no longer a part of their lives.
This can help the young people concerned to keep a sense of their
own identity but it may leave the adults involved feeling left out
or confused. The temptation is to charge in, renaming them and
insisting on the children calling you the name you would like to
have and feel most comfortable with, without considering exactly
how that feels to them. Many adults in new families argue that
changing the child's surname or insisting on their calling a new
adult Mum or Dad is for the child's good, as a way of creating
stability. If you were to be honest with yourself, the fact is that
this is more for your own emotional stability than theirs. You
may want to be Mum or Dad, Uncle or Auntie and this may
satisfy your needs, but the bitter truth is that however well this
sits with you, if it impacts against their needs, you are likely to
have arguments. The key lies in recognising honestly when what
you are proposing is actually a matter of feelings – your feelings
– rather than their feelings, or what seems right, or socially
acceptable. Deirdre, for instance, says:

*It's always been difficult knowing quite how to describe my
relationship to Paul. James and I have been together for 18 years*

and we've a permanent, stable partnership. But we've never actually married, so Paul isn't my stepson, not officially, and I'm not his stepmother. He once introduced me to a schoolfriend's mother as James's 'flatmate'. I do sometimes refer to him as my stepson because it's so complicated to have to go through the rigmarole of explaining. But I sometimes feel awkward as if I might be claiming a relationship with him that he might not want to acknowledge. I have a feeling that the fact that he didn't call either of his parents mum and dad all the time did help. He calls them and refers to them by their own first names. In fact, he never really calls James dad – unless he's taking the mickey and calling him Pater. So it seemed less of a glaring addition to have 'Deirdre' added to Laura and James. In fact, he calls me Dree, which has become his own special pet name for me, more often than Deirdre.

It may not only be adults and children who have differing and often opposite ideas of what is happening in a new family. Men and women often have very different ideas about whether a blended family is working and whether or not they feel comfortable within it. Being a stepmother may seem, on the surface, easier than being a stepfather, because the role of a mother is better defined in this society than that of a father. Mothers 'mother' – that is, they cook, clean, clothe and care for children. It can be simple for a woman to go through the motions of what everyone thinks of as mothering, and to define herself, and have everyone around her define her, as doing the job properly. When Sandra started living with Bill she was determined to be a good stepmother.

When his children first came to us for a weekend, they were in a dreadful state. Their mother is a bit of a slut so they'd turn up for the weekend in dirty clothes, without a clean change, and it was awful. I'd ask Bill to speak to her but he wasn't keen on doing it and anyway, he didn't quite see it as a problem. So, the third time it happened, I went out and bought them new outfits. I keep them

*here, so they have something nice to wear when they're with us. If I
sent them back wearing my clothes, she'd only mess them up so I
clean up the clothes they come in on Friday night and they go back
dressed in them on Sunday.*

Sandra genuinely believes that her behaviour is for the children's
good. She's surprised and upset, therefore, that the kids are sullen
and unappreciative and seem to take a delight in tearing and
soiling their nice, new clothes. The conflict springs from the fact
that she's only viewing the situation from her own viewpoint, in
which her need to 'do better' than Bill's first wife, and perhaps to
justify the break-up, is uppermost. The more she tries to replace
their mum, and the more she tries to impress Bill and the children
with her superior skills and care, the more upset the children
become.

WOMEN VOICE CONCERNS MORE OFTEN THAN MEN

It is significant that in spite of the fact that most step-parents are
fathers, it is stepmothers and birth mothers who usually ask for
help or voice any disquiet at what is happening within a blended
family. Men frequently have a rosier view about what is
happening than do the women involved. Whether the children
involved in a blended family are his or hers, and whether they live
with the couple part-time or full-time, it is often the woman who
actually looks after them, not the father. When young children
from a first marriage are sent to 'see Dad' this often means seeing
the new wife or partner, while Dad is out at work. This can be the
cause of deep resentment and cause conflict between adult and
child and adult and adult. It is probably why it is usually the
women who worry about what is happening within the family and
therefore have the greatest feelings of guilt and inadequacy about
blended families. Fewer stepmothers are in paid employment than

natural mothers, a result of their making a greater effort to be more like 'real' mothers than real mothers are. A stepmother who 'plays mum' in an attempt to be even better at the job than the birth mother may do more than alienate the children and the parent she is trying to replace. The children involved may become resentful of what they see as attempts to take over the 'real' mother's role, leaving her to feel particularly rejected and hurt because in her eyes she has been trying her best to give them what they need. But she also allows the man to be let off the hook. He can play less of a role within the blended family than he might otherwise have done, thinking that a parental presence is fully met by his non-working partner. As well as simply being with the children more than he, women tend to deal most with the emotional life of a family, even when the children are his.

By two years after the divorce, 50 percent of men have ceased having any contact with the family they left. Breakdown often occurs because a father's relationship with his child is frequently carried out *through* their mother. In this society men are often seen, and see themselves, primarily as money-earner and authority figure. Men are the head of the family while women are its heart. Mother, in other words, has the emotional link to the children and Dad rides in on her coat tails. When their relationship breaks up, the link is broken. He then has to try to establish a new, direct link between himself and his children without their mother as his interpreter and mediator. If this is attempted in the teeth of her opposition, the connection can be fragile or never even get going. Fathers often lose touch because they may not know how to relate to children directly on their own.

Two years after a divorce one in two men no longer have contact with the family they left.
Fathers lose touch because they may not know how to relate to children on their own.

Mothers tend to feel and operate as mothers even when they are apart from their children. When a mother leaves her children, she is still conscious of their link and can fight to retain it, even when a separation continues. Carolyn left her six-year-old son with her husband when she left him.

I walked out because of his violence and I got to snapping point. One day I suddenly realised I couldn't take it any more but I also knew that if I hesitated for a moment, I'd never have the courage to go. The only place I had to go to at such short notice was a friend's place and she only had room for me. So I left Kenny because his father had never been violent with him and I knew he was safe. It was the worst mistake I've ever made because he used it to apply for custody and barred me from seeing my son for almost 10 years. I remarried and had two children by my second husband but I never stopped thinking of Kenny and I never stopped fighting to get him back. Now he's 18, he's come to stay and I'm glad to say all the things his father said about me haven't succeeded in driving us apart. I never stopped thinking about him or wanting to have him back in all that time.

Many women do give up after a time, although, like Carolyn, they may continue to remember their children and hope for contact. This is most unlikely to be because of any inherent difference between men and women but rather because the two sexes are brought up to see parenting as a female job. The result is that fathers frequently see fatherhood as only having any meaning when they are with their children, so the less they see their children, the more fatherly feelings are likely to wane.

A strong indicator of whether or not a father may be able to stay in touch is his self-image and self-esteem and how well he might have got on with his own father. Men whose own fathers had good relationships with them have learnt, from example, how fathers and sons can have a bond. Those who have had a poor link with their own fathers may simply have no idea how fathering is done and these early experiences can leave a man feeling uncertain about his abilities to be a good parent. Men who feel they have some self-worth, even if the marital breakdown is painful and difficult, feel able to face the discomfort of keeping in touch.

THE MEANING OF FATHERHOOD

Not only do many men have little example to follow when learning how to be a dad, they often have quite negative images about traditional fatherhood. When the relationship between a father and his children by a former marriage is going well, they are likely to describe it in terms of friendship, often saying, 'He's more like a mate than a son,' and forgetting that a child doesn't want or need a friend, they want and need a father. If you remember your own dad as being a remote, distant authority figure, you may want to distance yourself from the role if being a father is to be like that. Fathers who do lose contact often see this as a noble sacrifice and persuade themselves that one day there will be a reconciliation. Kofi, for instance, has three children whom he left with his first wife when they separated. He has not seen them for five years but is convinced he will be reconciled with them when they are older.

She can't forgive me for leaving, especially since her family are old-fashioned and don't agree with divorce. She told me she would never let me see them again and would tell them I was an evil person. Well, that's sad but when they are older they'll be able to make up their own minds about the matter. I'm sure they'll give me a chance. It's not worth trying now but when they are 18 or 20 or near then, I will contact them and I'm sure they'll be pleased to see me.

Sadly, the longer children and parents are out of touch, the wider the gap there will be between them and the less likely they are to get back together. But fighting for control of children, disguised as a continuing battle for contact, can sometimes be as bad as no contact at all. It can be a particularly vicious dead end in a divided family and have lasting effects on any new family. When Sunny told her boyfriend Sherman that their relationship was finished and she was leaving with their son Duanne, he was furious.

I told her she couldn't do that, take a man's son and go for good. She told me since we'd never married I had no hold on him and she also said I wasn't a fit father. I know I'm no angel and I'd been seeing someone else, but it was over. Well, I've been to a solicitor and I want to take her to court and we'll see.

Since their separation, Sherman has made no attempt to see his son and refused Sunny's efforts to discuss access to him. All he has done is keep up a stream of threatening letters, saying he's going to take her to court for custody. Duanne misses him but Sherman does not answer any of the boy's letters or phone calls.

Fatherhood is often seen in terms of control and of issues of power. When we tell misbehaving children, 'Just wait till your father gets home!', we are underlining the belief that dad is the one who wields the authority at home – but, sadly, also saying that this is all he does. The result, often, is that men feel the only way they can go on being 'good' and 'proper ' fathers once their first family has split up is by having the whip hand and being in charge. Fathers who fight, who opt to go to court over access and control of their children as a *first* option, are often the ones who had least closeness with their children before a split and have least contact after. This is not always, as you might think, because going to court is their only resort against a hostile other parent. It may instead be because they see the loss of their children in terms of a loss of control, and using power and authority is seen by them as the best way to get it back. Sadly, what is actually lost when parents lose touch with their children is intimacy, normality, routine and love. The more the courts and authority are used in battles over access and authority, the less human contact is possible because these institutions do not foster love or relationships. Those fathers who communicate with the other parent and together work out a way of sharing parenting are often better at letting go of bitterness. Adults can communicate and be co-parents even when they have ceased loving each other and even when they are no longer friends.

The reason that men, whether natural fathers or stepfathers, often have an unrealistic picture of what is happening, either within the family they might have left or within their reconstituted family, is because they believe their main role exists outside the family home. Children and women are often the ones to bear the brunt of any difficulties at home. For example, both Alec's father and his mother's new partner think he has adjusted well to their arrangement, which is that Alec lives with his mother, stepfather and their two children. His father has gradually stopped seeing him, saying he feels the boy has accepted the new family and that it would be unfair on all of them to 'keep dragging up the past'. His mother recognises that Alec fights with his younger half brothers, and hates his stepfather's two daughters, who visit every weekend. She also knows the reason he avoided seeing his father and sulked every time he did so was nothing to do with being happy at 'home' but because his father's new wife ignored him and made him feel unwelcome. Both the men have laughed off any suggestion that Alec is unhappy, however, and neither will discuss the situation at all. The reason, perhaps, that neither will focus on Alec's point of view is that it conflicts with their own. Both adults here feel comfortable and more at ease 'leaving well alone'. Understanding that the boy may have different feelings from their own means acknowledging his unhappiness and having to face up to it. Many of us would rather not do that.

The expectation that it is mothers who care for children means that when a woman leaves her children, she may feel more guilt, come under more pressure and be faced with far more hostility than a father who goes, as Carolyn found.

It was the worst thing I could have done, leaving my son, because even my own parents and sisters went over to my husband's side. As far as everyone was concerned, I'd abandoned my child and that made me unfit to have him. My mum has never really forgiven me but she gets on fine with him and his new wife. They all forgot about what my husband did to me and all they ever went on about was what I had done to my son, leaving him. When I tried to get him back, the social workers supported his father, especially after he remarried and when I went to court, the magistrate believed this lawyer who made out that I was some kind of monster, that I'd abandoned him, not that I'd left my husband because of his violence. In fact, when I remarried and we had a baby, we got a visit from a social worker. It seems, they had me marked down as a mum who wouldn't look after her kids properly.

GETTING IT RIGHT SECOND TIME AROUND

As well as the need for step-parents to prove themselves better at both partnering and parenting than the person whose place they are taking, someone in a second relationship may want to prove they can do better this time than they did the last time. Driven by having 'failed' at the first marriage, they may hope to succeed at being a good partner and parent, and to want to put aside any hint of what has gone before. In a second relationship it's very easy to cherish unrealistically high expectations from a new partner and a new marriage as well as from yourself. There may be the unreasonable double demand that not only does the new arrangement have to be the perfect marriage but that it should somehow have the magical power to cure all the hurt and remove all the complications of the previous one. Jealousy is a major hazard of second families, rooted as it always is in insecurity. Secure people do not feel jealous. They may feel envious or resentful but they do not suffer the fear that the person they love prefers someone else, that someone has or is going to take what is theirs away from them. In a second relationship, the proof exists that someone other than you was there first and, with children in the equation, there is always that conflict of loyalties to pull one of you away. If you have not come to this blended family with your confidence and your self-esteem in good order, it may be easy to slide into negative thoughts.

The key to making it work often lies in looking for the positive aspect. Whether children become a full-time or a part-time presence in your life, they will have a considerable effect. This can actually be enormously beneficial if handled sensitively. Perhaps the most helpful advice given by people who have made it work is not to try to make the family a replacement for 'the real thing', not to pretend that the situation is that of birth parents and birth children, but something new and different As a step-parent, don't aim to be a second-class parent but a first-class significant other.

Clearly a new partner will have taken the place of one parent in the other parent's life and this still may be a lingering cause for resentment and jealousy in the children's eyes. But if they do not try to replace the parent in the child's life, both the child and the other birth parent may be able to see the situation in constructive terms. Some parents have found their ex's new partner is able to fulfil a role in their children's lives that is a positive asset. Living with a new 'step' can be a lot better than living with a single parent, who might be lonely and bitter otherwise. It isn't always doom and gloom and the truth is that some children come to a step-parent with a sigh of relief and find a special relationship with them that takes an enormous amount of pressure off their own parents. Making the presence of children, and their other parent, a bonus rather than a drawback, making an effort rather than ignoring them, can help you to cope with the situation.

DIFFERENT ROLES

It's very hard to ignore the existence of children in a new relationship. You can start off on the wrong foot from day one, simply because privacy and the opportunity to be together can be hard to find. But wanting to be alone may not be the only reason that children from a former relationship might be felt to blight a new one. The other may be a conflict between being a parent at the same time as being a lover. All of us fulfil many roles at any one time in our lives. We are parents to our own children at the same time as being a child to our own parents; husbands and wives at the same time as being fathers and mothers. When we try to run more than one role side-by-side, and particularly when the roles are contradictory, stress and tension can result. Most of us have felt the awkwardness of being bossed around and coddled by our parents while trying to do exactly the same thing to our own children, and it can make us snappish with both generations.

Asif finds himself becoming particularly annoyed with his own parents now he has married for the second time.

They've always been ones to make a fuss of me. I used to be embarrassed to take my first wife to see them sometimes. We met at university but the way my mother went on, you'd think I was still in nursery school. I suppose most parents are like that and I put up with it but now it is beyond a joke. I'm a grown man with three children yet when we see them she goes on at me, whether I'm eating properly or working too hard. It's as if my wife and our new baby, and our other children, just don't exist. I have to be a son to them, a father to my children and a new husband to my wife and sometimes I feel as if my head is spinning. I used to drop in to see my parents a couple of times a week and now, it's more like every other month, if that. It's just too much hard work.

The clash between conflicting roles is even stronger when roles that don't usually coincide are brought together. You don't expect to be in the full throes of a new love affair at the same time as being a mum or a dad. Compromise is really very difficult, and in many cases children suffer because you invest so much energy into the new marriage that their needs are neglected. In others, the new relationship has to take a back seat to the effort of keeping the children happy and secure.

A common complaint of adults in a stepfamily is that the children involved cause more arguments and unhappiness than found in 'normal' family life. We can easily forget that original parents in a conventional family argue and disagree with their own children, and don't always find their behaviour acceptable. We never think to ask or wonder whether we 'get on' with our own children the way we often agonise about how we fit in with children in a blended family, or they fit in with us. Birth parents don't like their children all the time but adults in a blended family often demand more of themselves than they would a birth parent. A step-parent can have feelings of guilt, failure and even of being evil if he or she doesn't like their partner's children. With all these unhappy feelings flying about, it is easy to see how they have to come to earth somewhere. Everyone has a justified reason for feeling bitter and angry at someone else in the pattern. One way of dealing with these unhappy feelings is to 'project' them on to the child concerned. Projection is when we take our own 'bad' feelings about a thing or person and credit them to someone else. We feel angry or jealous about a child, but feel that it is really quite monstrous that we should have such strong, destructive feelings about an innocent, harmless, little object. The feelings still exist, so we tell ourselves that it's the child who has these feelings for us, and perhaps by being angry and/or jealous themselves, the child really deserves our anger or jealousy back. So, it is the child who is the monster, not us or our feelings. Self-protectively, we then see evil, calculation and viciousness in everything the child does.

When Maria met Carlo, she was charmed by his two sons.

They live with their mother but he sees them every weekend. I thought they were fine until we said we were getting married. Then the eldest became big trouble. He's horrible, calling me names and sulking every time they see me. He once tipped paint all over the living room carpet, just to upset me. I can't stand them but Carlo can't see how awful they are. He wants me to try harder.

Carlo came for help, asking that the counsellor tell Maria that she should be kinder to the boys.

But it's not me that needs to change – I didn't do anything!

she insists. Neither is happy about discussing why Carlo wants Maria to look after his children when they come to stay, why Maria thinks the boys deliberately needle her and how the boys might be feeling. Carlo seems to feel so bad about the break-up of his first marriage that he finds it hard to face his boys, who take out their feelings of hurt and rejection on Maria. Maria, in her turn, was the eldest child in an Italian family that idolised the next baby, a boy. When she and the counsellor looked at her family tree, it seemed to suggest that all her angry feelings for her brother were coming out against Carlo's older boy, who reminds her of her brother. But she and Carlo found counselling so challenging that soon after this, they stopped coming.

THE BLACK SHEEP OF THE FAMILY?

A new partner implicated in the break-up of a relationship or marriage will almost certainly become a scapegoat for the discarded partner, any children and the relatives, often of both families. This desire to blame someone and to find a target for the concern and confusion felt in the aftermath of a disintegrated relationship will often mean that even a new partner who had nothing to do with the breakdown is still blamed. This is also

! ——————————— *Task* ———————————

Family roles

We've all heard them, and we've all done it: 'Sheila? Oh, she's always been the joker in our family'. or, 'You're just like your Uncle Fred, he was a rebel too'. Sometimes the labels seem complimentary, 'Who's Mummy's little helper?' or, 'He's such a good child, never gives me any bother'. Sometimes they are more damaging, 'Your father was a no-good and you'll end up like just him'.

Imagine the roles in a family being like a set of fancy dress costumes for a party. It's as if these have to go round, and everybody must be dressed in one. Nice or nasty, you put your costume on and then you're stuck with it. Sometimes you pick your own costume. Even though you want to change later, you may find nobody else can see you in any other way. Sometimes, you find you've had your costume chosen for you and you grow to fit it.

Look at these words. Can you find descriptions that fit you and your own family? Can you add any more words?

Mother's little helper	Dreamer
Good child	Sulker
Bad child	Little Princess
Rebel	The Little Madam
Tomboy	Hard Worker
Joker	Ne'er-do-well
Lazy one	

Look at the roles occupied by you and your blended family. Which roles are held by which people? Do you think these people are comfortable in them? Who says they suit their label? Do they really fit? Would you or they prefer not to wear their role? How can you change?

!

why sometimes we only feel upset about one of several children. We may tell ourselves, and others, that this particular child has qualities or behaviour that make them difficult but the real reason is that we have chosen them to bear the brunt of our emotions. Having become a scapegoat and having acquired the label of being 'bad', a child may decide he or she has no choice but to behave badly and live up to the role we have given them.

We always like to imagine that our own feelings and behaviour are beyond reproach and that if we are stung to anger or complaint it is for a very good reason. When approaching the pain and the difficulties that can be found in a blended family you shouldn't underestimate the role of your own less savoury or unacceptable feelings, such as envy and jealousy. Adults, having a position of power in a family, often consider their own feelings to be beyond discussion or reproach. Paul, now 26, lived with his mother until he went to college, seeing his father James and partner Deirdre on weekends and during holidays.

Children don't always understand that their parents will be feeling the same as them – jealous, guilty, hurt, etc. It took me quite a long time to understand that though my mother likes my father, she is jealous and upset to see him enjoying a level of relationship with his new partner that she would like herself. Her hurt is not caused by Deirdre, but by seeing a situation she wants, one that she also envies friends for having, except that the involvement of an ex-husband probably makes it more extreme. I finally realised this, I'm not so sure she has. She tended to say he was being selfish or unreasonable or jerking me about when he didn't fall in with what she wanted us to do. I think, in retrospect, she wasn't aware how much her own feelings were getting in the way.

6

SHOWING HOW YOU FEEL

Step-families are often more economically disadvantaged than 'natural' families of a similar type. This may be because, in many cases, the men involved are also paying for their first family, and stepmothers often do not work. Money is often the main cause of conflict in second marriages. It is easy to see why this is so. A divorced wife can claim an increase in maintenance for her children if her ex-husband's situation changes. If he remarries, and his second wife works, while her income and her assets are not counted as his, what will be taken into account is her contribution to his second family. He is not ordered to pay more simply because his new wife is well off. The assumption is that if her income relieves him of having to maintain his new family alone, so more of his money can be released for his first family. Similarly, if his first wife remarries into affluence it may not mean the end of his responsibilities because the law expects him to pay for the maintenance of his children, not for her. It is worth noting in these days of equality that both parents are considered to be responsible for their children. If it is the mother who has left and the father who is caring for their children, she may be the one who is expected to contribute and she may find herself in precisely the same situation.

Every single member of the step-family, both adults and children, may feel they have good cause to resent money that is demanded of them, given by them or appears to be owed to them. As in so many situations, arguments of this type are usually a way of skirting round the real issue, which is about your real needs not being met. Rows about money are really to do with something else. When you are overwhelmed with anger about the other person's stinginess or feel they're not giving you enough cash, what you are actually saying is that they've taken or you've lost something that you value – their love and attention. That is actually what you want back, and you try to fill the hole by asking them to give you money. Demands that could cause real hardship to the other parent may be justified with the thought, 'he's only getting his just deserts', because what you want is to know they are experiencing as much pain and hurt in paying up as you might have felt at losing them. When members of a new family complain or feel upset about the money that is being spent on children or an ex-spouse, the fear again is symbolic: that giving money to the other family means it is still loved and may be more important than the new one. Giving lavishly is sometimes a way of overcompensating for guilt. Instead of facing up to the grief involved in the disruption of the original family, one parent will throw money at it as a way of paying off their obligations and in order to walk away with a clear conscience. Since money is never a good substitute for the love, care and attention, everyone involved tends to go on feeling a loss, and go on making demands.

Money is often used to show how you feel
about a separation and a new family.

Money becomes a flashpoint because it is a symbol. It is a convenient means by which an abandoned spouse can continue to vent his or her anger, pain and bitterness upon the other person after a marriage has broken down. Money may be used to continue the power play that existed in a relationship before a separation. Hannah was left by her husband, who remarried a younger woman, leaving their six-year-old son with her.

He was generous with money after he left me. It took me some time to realise that I was dancing to his tune as much after our divorce as I always had before he left me. I married him instead of going to university and was pregnant two months later. He never let me have a job, never let me go on with my education and it was the same after we divorced. He never said it but I knew if I worked or went back to college, it would be goodbye to the comfortable life he was financing. It was five years before I had the guts to make a stand. I applied to do a degree as a mature student and three weeks later, the letter from his solicitor came. He'd go on paying for the upkeep of our son but if I went ahead, he would assume I no longer needed any contribution to my own maintenance. I actually sat there for an hour, thinking it over before realising we were divorced and it was time for me to make my own choices. After all, he was the one who left, not the other way round, but I think he always wanted to keep a connection between us and holding my purse strings was the only way he could do it.

Hannah made the decision to break the ties between herself and her first husband and started her college course. Her husband would periodically be in touch and often changed arrangements to see their son or sent unpleasant, slighting messages through him. She saw a counsellor at her college, and with his support, realised these were the only ways he now saw to retain control of her, which obviously satisfied some need of his. Hannah shrugged off his influence which she came to recognise she no longer wanted or needed, and took her degree. She eventually started a career in the media and three years later, married again.

Money may also be used by the parent who leaves or the one with whom a child lives, as a means of trying to maintain the often fragile connection between parent and children. James did not see his son Paul according to a regular schedule, but there were frequent visits. On some of these, Paul's mother would make requests that would spark resentment in James and his partner Deirdre.

What did upset me was the way she would send Paul for a weekend with a list of clothes to buy. We were broke and she had a good job and her family was pretty comfortably off and very supportive. At the time, I just couldn't see why she needed to make these demands, that James felt unable to refuse. We would get the clothes, with Paul choosing what he wanted, and as far as we'd know, he'd never wear them again! At least, he'd never come and see us in them. He always wore the same old army surplus and jeans. Now, perhaps, I understand the pressures on him and on her. Money is such a symbol, and it was important for both of them to see James proving he still cared. But I'd get furious and I suppose it wasn't really the money itself but the feeling it was making unfair demands and taking something away from us. Stupid really, but very real at the time.

Money can also be used by members of a wider family network to underline their feelings of who does and does not belong inside the family proper. Gifts may be unequal or withheld almost as a way of saying that a particular child does not exist in their eyes. Paula, who remarried and had a baby with a man 18 years older than her, found his mother very resistant to her two children from her first marriage.

Christmas is an absolute nightmare because she showers her own grandchildren with presents, and that's including our baby, but ignores my two. They may be living with Scott but they're nothing to do with her, as far as she's concerned. Last year they had to stand there and watch while she gave the baby, and Scott's three grown up children and their children, loads of gifts and they were tossed a packet of sweets each – yes, really!

Paula wrote to me, asking for help with dealing with presents over Christmas and I suggested she and Scott talk it over first. As I said, the first step may be to ask the family to treat all children in your blended family the same and explain that you won't stand for divisiveness, but both partners need to be united in this instance. Of course, you need to take the same message on board yourself and not treat your 'own' children differently from any new children of the blended family. If they can't or won't play fair, it would be time to sit down with your family to talk over what is going on. You'd need to get your partner to agree a strategy for dealing with this pressure and to explain to the children that it isn't their fault. Paula and Scott were both agreed and did tackle his mother but she avoided talking for some time. When they finally insisted, she became angry at first and then upset. The following Easter, she gave all three children the same size Easter egg. Paula thanked her and got her two to write pretty cards thanking her too. Some time later, Scott's mother told him how she could remember as a child her brother, the baby of her family, being spoiled while she got very little. As is so common, people often behave unfairly because they themselves have been subjected to unfair treatment. Once she had recognised what she was doing and been asked to face up to the pain it caused, Scott's mother did change.

BUYING LOVE

Generosity, genuine or apparent, on the part of the non-resident partner can be just as much a weapon as meanness. The parent who has less contact may want to 'spoil' the child, as a way of buying loyalty or even of forcing a wedge between the child and the full-time and possibly less well off parent. But they may also be heaping material goods on the child in an attempt to make up for the vital element they feel they have taken from the child – a stable family. Both guilt and competitiveness are at the root of many family and relationship problems, and never more than in blended families. When Steve and his first wife split up and he married Sue, he tried to keep in contact with all three of his children.

I couldn't go on living with her, the marriage wasn't working for either of us and it was miserable. But I loved my children and felt just awful for leaving. I suppose I went through a bad phase when I just threw money at it, buying them presents all the time but constantly letting them down and not keeping to arrangements. The truth was I couldn't always face them, I felt so bad about the break up. My ex was angry enough when I left but she got more and more bitter and I can't really blame her. I'd have the kids going back to her saying, 'Why can't you buy us this and that, Dad does?' It made me feel better that I was good for something in their lives but in the long run it just made things worse. The sad thing is that now I've got myself sorted out more and I'd like to have a better relationship with her and all my children but it seems a bit late. My son comes and stays with me but he no longer talks to his mum and the girls won't see me any more.

Tragically, using money or any other form of emotional blackmail to remind everyone concerned that the estranged parent is or should be still responsible and involved often goes wrong.

TRYING TO GET IT RIGHT

Once the dust has settled, some parents who have left a former partner and their children may feel matters have been resolved enough to make a new beginning with their kids. It's not uncommon for a leaving parent suddenly to take great interest in their children and actually become a better parent at a distance than they were as full-time carers. This may feel right to them, but if there is unfinished business left over for the parent with whom the children live, it can cause enormous resentment in them and any other adult in the blended family. Angie and Martin divorced after three years of marriage and their son Bob lives with Angie and her new husband, Tony.

It really gets me furious, and Tony as well. Martin never paid the kid a moment's notice when he was born and I had to do everything when he was a baby. Now we're split up, Martin thinks he can swan in at any time and act like a dad. He seems to think we should all be grateful or something, give him prizes for being Number 1 Dad and it makes me sick. He wasn't like this before, he was rubbish as a father, so what's his game now?

If you are the parent (usually the mother) who has borne the brunt of bringing up the child even before the break-up, you may be unable to be happy either for your child or the other parent at this new interest in the child's well-being. You may feel cheated by the leaving parent who has avoided most of the work of parenting, but now apparently gets all the fun and the praise, particularly when the children return from visits full of happy tales of adventure and play. It might seem as if the part-time parent does have all the good times and none of the bad. Full-time parents, because of anger and resentment, may then want to have some control over the relationship the child has with the part-time parent, and what they do together. Many full-time parents want to know exactly what their ex-spouses do with the children on contact meetings, and become critical. Angie complains:

He takes the boy every Saturday but now I find he takes him round his mum's and leaves him there while he plays football in the afternoon. That's not right. Why should he be with them? And surely if he's going to see the boy, he should be seeing him and not larking about with his mates?

What Angie is unwilling to recognise is that this sort of normal, everyday contact with his father – and, indeed, his grandparents – is exactly what Bob needs and likes. Making some sort of a special effort to be together every minute of the day would feel forced and strained. Leaving the child with his parents is Martin's way of keeping up the sort of family life he would have enjoyed if he had remained with his son. Martin plans to take Bob along to watch him play when the boy is old enough, as he would have if he had been a full-time father but at the moment, he needs his own parents' help in keeping the link. As already mentioned, many father/child relationships go through the mother, who either makes, eases and encourages this contact or controls, limits and obstructs it. When parents split up, some fathers may not be able to maintain the relationship on their own without the help of a woman, in the shape of a new partner or their own mother. When they do, for the first time, develop their own links, the ex-partner may feel this threatens her position as first in her children's affections, and resent it. What Angie finds hardest to own up to is that Bob looks forward to his Saturdays, and it is his approval that may most fuel her anger. Sadly, a split between parent and parent might endanger both parents' link with their children. It is common for children and their parents to have disagreements. When one parent and a particular child are at loggerheads, the other parent may find him or herself playing mediator and healing the breach. When natural parents live in different households, not only may one not attempt to act as go-between when there is friction, he or she may delight in and encourage the argument. The resultant bad feeling, which often lasts, can affect everyone in both families.

When Janifa and Olly divorced, Olly continued to see his son Lee and daughter Bonnie until he and Lee had an argument.

We always had words, me and Lee. We're too much alike and now he's a teenager there were always dust-ups. But they tended to get smoothed over when we lived together. Janny would make the peace in the end and it would blow over. She says it's up to me now since I was the one to leave and he won't talk to me. Bonnie comes and sees me but she says every time she says anything, her mum tells her to leave it alone and let us sort it out. But I can't. He won't speak on the phone and if I go round, he won't come out of his room. It's been going on two years now and I've hardly seen him.

Bonnie says the whole thing is getting to Janny's new man, too. Marc says he's getting fed up with the rows and may move out.

DISCIPLINE

If there are children in your second family, who gets to tell them what to do can become one of the flashpoints for conflict. Disciplining children is one of the most difficult areas of parenting in any family, and never more so than in a reconstituted one. Many people label themselves, and others, as good or bad parents on the basis of how well-behaved children appear and whether the adults in a family are in control. When control is an issue and you feel uncertain about your ability to take charge, children are most likely to challenge you and create conflict. You may find yourself swinging between the two extremes of being overpermissive and avoiding making any demands because you feel they have already suffered so much, to being particularly firm because you don't want to be accused of not being a proper parent. Anyone starting out in a second relationship may be suffering a lack of self-esteem and a lack of self-confidence which makes the subject of discipline of especial concern. When the children involved are not your own, knowing how, when and where to draw the line can be further complicated by a genuine uncertainty as to whether you have the right to tell these children what to do. To understand why discipline is such a problem for step-families you have to understand what discipline is for in any family. Perhaps the purpose most often quoted when you ask parents why they need to have control over their children, is to protect young people from doing anything that could hurt them. This can cover preventing crawling babies from sticking their fingers into electric sockets right up to asking teenagers to be home soon after dark so they don't get run over, mugged or assaulted. Delve a bit deeper and you'll realise the second, and actually more important, role is to teach them

! ———————————————— *Task* ————————

What's the trigger?

We often find ourselves in violent arguments that seem to blow up out of nowhere, and reach astounding levels of aggression. Sometimes, afterwards, we realise our response was out of proportion to the offence but we often feel powerless to understand or stop what happened. This is an exercise to help you to work out:

WHAT MAKES YOU ANGRY

WHY IT HAPPENS

WHEN IT HAPPENS

The question to ask yourself is 'What's the button and what pushes it?' The next time you get angry, sit down afterwards. You might get a friend or your partner to do this exercise with you, if talking it over with someone else helps. Remember what made you angry. Think about when you've felt like that before. What were your feelings when you became angry? What were you doing to deal with those feelings? Did it work?

Lillian, for instance, would get angry with her husband Sandile and his son Jake. She said it was because Jake would be sullen and ungrateful and Sandile didn't help the situation. Every time Jake came to stay, it ended in an argument between the three of them that then went on for days between her and Sandile. When Lillian did this exercise she realised that what pushed her buttons was Jake becoming quiet, as he always did at the end of his time with them. She realised that when he did this, she began to feel anxious. And when she felt anxious, she became angry and blamed Jake. When she closed her eyes and thought about these feelings, she found herself back as a small child. Her father had worked away from home and every Sunday night, Lillian had been sent to bed knowing he would be gone in the morning until next Friday night. The feelings she had with Jake were the same as those she had then – grief, loss and fear. Her feelings of powerlessness were so great that she became angry with the person who stirred these uncomfortable feelings in her (Jake) and with Sandile, who reminded her of her father. Lillian's anger was mainly misplaced, leftover anger from her own childhood. Once she realised WHAT, WHY, WHEN, she found she could cope with the feelings she had and that they became far less destructive.

Once you begin to recognise your own buttons, and what pushes them, you can begin to deal with them too.

!

manners and self-control – to socialise them and prepare them to be acceptable members of the community. But all theory aside, the real, immediate and arguably the most necessary reason for discipline is to stop children doing something that drives you up the wall and round the bend!

In a blended family you may have confused and conflicting feelings about the safety, manners and behaviour of the children and adults, involved. Whether you admit it or not, you might have mixed feelings about their safety. All parents and partners have moments when they wish the ground would open and swallow up the other members of a family. In most blended families this wish is less easy to admit to precisely because it is so often greatly desired. Since most step-parents find themselves at some time or other having horrible fantasies about their step-children being hurt or even being 'removed,' when danger does threaten them you may react with extra fear and rage. This is another form of 'projection'. The reality may be too uncomfortably close to what you've secretly, guiltily, wished would happen. So, you'll feel angry with yourself for having imagined it and rather than accept and recognise these uncomfortable feelings, you'll direct your anger on to the child.

After all, you'll reason to yourself, they're the ones who almost walked under a car or stuck their fingers in the electric socket – it's their fault and being punished will teach them a lesson!

> Young people respond best
> to being praised for getting it right
> rather than being told off for getting it wrong.

Another reason why discipline is so important in a blended family is that you want so much for it to appear 'normal' that you can't risk the children 'showing you up'. You'll forget that birth parents and their children in an original family frequently clash. You'll feel that any situation where you appear not to be in control underlines the fact that yours is not a normal, happy family. The chances are that the demands you make of them could well be unrealistic. You might be seeing indiscipline and the need for a stern hand in what could actually be normal, harmless childhood behaviour that requires nothing more than tolerance. It's not actually their behaviour that drives you up the wall – it's their very existence. What we, as adults and parents, often forget is that young people respond best to being asked and given choices rather than told; to being praised for getting it right rather than being told off for getting it wrong; to being respected rather than being directed.

You will need to sort out your rules, your values and your standards between yourself and the children and between yourself and the other adults concerned. Discuss your views on discipline and behaviour within and outside the home. It obviously helps if these are both similar and consistent and you can come to an agreement. You may well find, however, that you have differences and this is not necessarily a problem as long as you understand where you diverge, agree to differ and explain this to all concerned. When there are variations in what you demand and expect of yourselves and others in the family, it is important not to undermine each other. Comparisons are odious, even if irresistible. If you must dwell on the differences between parents and households to the children or other relatives, at least do so without making this a judgement, but a reflection. You can present children, and indeed other adults, with a valuable lesson in life that people can disagree on behaviour even though they have the same priority, which is a concern for their well-being. Whether you are in agreement or not, it's helpful for children living full-time or part-time with you if you make the ground rules clear.

Blended families frequently suffer from a crisis of identity and confidence. Neither new parent nor child may have a clear idea of what is expected from them or the relationship. Indeed, nobody may be sure who's in charge or who's responsible. In most birth-parent families, there's an understanding that both parents have a say in decision-making or discipline, even though the situation may be fudged at times. In a step-family there may be great confusion over who has the right to make suggestions and who has ultimate control.

Arguments can be provoked when children have to share time between households with a different parenting style. The child may resist rules set in one home because they feel they are losing the stability that comes with a known system. The problem is that all of us fall back on childish patterns when we are under stress, and you may equally need to cling to the conviction that what you are asking is right. After a divorce, it is inevitable that parents will grow apart and this may be reflected in the way you want to bring up your children. A new partner may bring fresh habits and ideas that appeal. The other parent may resent yet more proof that he or she has been thrown over for 'a better model' and dig their heels in, even when what they see going on between parent and child is a vast improvement on the past.

You can also start off badly if one of the adults is experiencing their first real contact with children. You are not born knowing how to be a parent, it's something you pick up by

! ================= *Task* =================

Responsibility brainstorm

Who in your family makes the decisions, does the work and has the say? Who, in other words, takes responsibility for what? Make this exercise a family discussion using 'brainstorming' to get you going. Brainstorming is when you say anything you want to say, within some guidelines. These are the same guidelines as for constructive argument outlined in Chapter 2. The most important rule is that everyone has to 'own' what they say. That means, you have to begin what you say with 'I think' or 'I feel'. No one can say, 'So-and-so says' or, 'Everyone knows', or talk about what other people do or what you think they think. You can talk about how other people's behaviour affects you, by saying, 'When you do such-and-such, I feel . . .' but the aim is to put your point of view, not to criticise or attack other people. Remember, the key is confronting problems, not people. You might like to go round the table letting each person say one thing, to start. Some families have a 'facilitator', who ensures that everyone takes it in turns to speak without interruption. If you do this, let everyone, from oldest to youngest, have a turn at being facilitator. Or, use an object to point out whose turn it is to speak and ask everyone only to talk when they have had it handed to them. No one is to be shouted down for what they say. Discuss the points rather than arguing with the person. Set aside time for the discussion and allow everyone a chance to speak, as many times as they like. You can't disagree with what someone says if they are explaining their feelings, however much you dislike or object to what is said or feel it is wrong or unfair. What you can do is say how it makes you feel to hear them say that! Take the opportunity to discuss it, understand why they feel that way, explain your side and see if everyone can come to an understanding.

Look at the list of areas of potential disagreement here. Can you add any more? Once you've completed the list, put a tick in the columns for who is in charge in your family at the moment – you can tick more than one column if the responsibility is shared.

	She	He	Kids	Exes	Other
Discipline					
Where you live					
Education					
Homework					
Meals and mealtimes					
Kids' friends					
Kids' clothes					
Contact with relatives					
Finances					
Leisure					
Bed times					
Holidays					
Feeding pets					
Doing chores					

Now, discuss whether you think this is fair and works for you. If not, who do you think should take responsibility for these? Fill in the chart again, using a different colour pen. Why would you like a change? Look at the areas you want to change and the ones you feel are OK.

!

watching how your own parents do it and then by practical experience with your own children. A new step-parent may come to it with little practical experience at all. They may then find themselves facing a step-child who has every reason to want to be critical, and who is old enough and articulate enough to be able to

! ———————————— *Task* ————————————

I love you because

If keeping contact with everyone involved in a second family overwhelms you, it's easy to let your one-to-one relationship suffer. You may believe that it will stand the test of time and pressure, while everything else demands immediate attention. Sadly, you find the two of you may lose out unless you spend some time and effort on your own relationship, whatever else you think needs your notice. Get back in touch by taking the time to remember that you love your partner, by talking about your reasons for this. Sit down with your partner and tell him or her:

What you first noticed about them

What attracted you first to them

What you liked doing with them when you first knew each other

What you miss doing and would like to do again

What you like doing now

What new thing you'd like to do with them

Make a date, this weekend or one evening this week, to do one of the things you miss doing from the past, like doing now or would like to try. Agree to do this exercise once a week in future. Take it in turns to choose something old or new to keep your relationship alive.

!

notice and comment on the step-parent's inexperience and uncertainty. In this society we do seem to place unreasonable emphasis on adult experience and infallibility and frown on the idea of an adult saying to a child, 'I haven't the foggiest idea!' So you are most likely to feel that you ought to know what you are doing and to collapse in an agony of self-recrimination, or explode in anger if a child sneers. The age of not only the new partner but of the children themselves can have some bearing on your feelings about them, and your role. A step-parent who is far younger than their partner or the parent whose place they are taking may feel particularly awkward and self-conscious. This may be less acute if the children are themselves very young but if they are old enough to make judgements and put their feelings into words or action, this may lead to conflict.

If you do have problems, it's very easy to blame this entirely on the fact that you are a blended family. You may have what is actually a typical parent/child or parent/adolescent disagreement and decide that it's the fault of being a blended family. Instead of taking the whole thing in your stride, realising that all families have these rows, you may worry yourself sick about your inadequacies or complain bitterly about the children's shortcomings. For example, all children will be rude or cheeky at times and will resist ordinary requests to do chores such as making beds or laying tables. In a 'normal' family, such behaviour should, and usually would, get short shrift. In a blended family, you may allow them to get away with it, either because you feel guilty for the hard time they've had or because you don't feel able to put your foot down. All children have passing moods and rebelliousness but this may touch such a raw nerve that you may explode in over-the-top rage. Adults in a blended family often notice every little sulk, snarl or pout in their children. They become convinced that such behaviour is the sign of deep confusion and depression and it's all their fault, while others who know them, such as teachers, might be more realistic in saying this is no more than normal, youthful moodiness.

7

OTHER PEOPLE HAVE FEELINGS, TOO

There will be two important influences at work when you approach a relationship where one or both of you has had a previous partner. The first comes from within you – your own needs and the way you respond to what happens in your life and in relationships. These needs and your reactions are often set into patterns by events in the past as much as by what occurs in the here and now. The other comes from those around you – your family and your friends, the community you live in and society at large. When we talk about our own point of view, we need to consider equally how the influences of other adults may affect our expectations of step-parenting, and how we perform the role. Whether you realise it or not, what other people think and believe affects the way you feel, act and behave. To understand what may happen when a restructured family comes together, we need to look at how outside pressures may influence us all.

Other adults will be as influenced by the messages they have received about family and their place in it as you have been. They, too, will be working from their own 'family script' and this could well lead to their having deep-seated and strong feelings about what they see in your life. Grandparents and in-laws may, deliberately or unwittingly, be at the heart of some of the problems in a new extended family. Relatives may not know how to respond to a new person, or they may respond in ways that are far from helpful. They may act as if the new adult, or the new children, are trespassers and interlopers, or they may overwhelm you and the new additions with a welcome that is suffocating. You may experience special difficulties if grandparents have actually looked after the children during the break-up of their parents' marriage or while the new relationship was being established. They may then feel they themselves have a role with the children which the newly involved adult usurps.

RELATIVES – WHO HELPS, WHO HINDERS?

Relatives may also be resentful if they feel the new adult or children exert a claim that is somehow fraudulent. Deirdre has found her mother's attitude towards her partner's son Paul particularly difficult.

My mother doesn't accept the relationship at all. She made it clear that she intends leaving her money to a trust fund with the interest going to me in my lifetime, but the capital to the trust. The point of that is to make absolutely sure that Paul, not being my real child, will not inherit her money, or possessions that are part of our family inheritance. I think that's awful, because I feel he is my family and I want him to have things that have a meaning to me, such as paintings that belonged to my grandmother. They have only met once, when she was polite and charming. But she never suggested another meeting and when I talk about him she makes no comment. When I told her recently that he had got a good degree, she said James must be pleased, but no more. She doesn't consider him my son, so she certainly doesn't see herself as even a quasi-grandmother. He is a stranger to her and nothing to do with her, she feels. My feelings about him have nothing to do with it. If I was married to James, she might feel differently. But without a legal tie, she sees no emotional tie.

Refusing to become involved or to recognise a relationship may be the tip of the iceberg. In many other families the attitudes and feelings of grandparents and others may be hostile and interfering. It is important not to ask anyone – your friends, your relatives, the children themselves – to take sides, but ask them to see all of you and your situation as common, natural and neutral. It may be helpful to ask the wider family to make an effort to do this and not to put undue extra pressure on an already delicate situation. If they won't or can't put aside their personal feelings, the best policy is to explain this to the children, so that they can understand that there are different opinions at large. Often, relatives or friends offer what they think is support, without bothering to check out whether it is welcomed by the people they want to help. Paul says:

It's very easy for even the most well meaning of relatives to 'take sides', when what you really want is to be cheered up. If your father or mother is beyond redemption, then that sort of behaviour may be fair enough. If they're not, then it's better for others to say nothing if they can't be constructive. Relatives' loyalty is to their side of the family rather than the success of the relationship. You can have people rushing in to bad-mouth your father and stick up for your mother and all that does is leave you feeling like s**t . I've sometimes felt I can't go to anyone for a shoulder to cry on when I'm down, because of this sort of attitude, and that doesn' t help at all.

Sometimes, the 'checking out' could go both ways. Those on the fringes may do nothing harmful but nothing helpful either, because you haven't asked them to. Kerry, who married a man 15 years older than her with three children, found most of his friends unhelpful, if not positively unfriendly.

I struggled on for ages, on my own, trying to be cool and OK about it all. George knew there was a problem but he didn't quite realise how much it hurt me. I didn't want to tell my parents. They're a bit remote and cold and my father always had very high expectations of me and I didn't want to let on I couldn't cope. The last people I thought of going to were George's family. Then his sister made a passing remark and we found out that while I thought they might not have been supportive, they were but they thought I hadn't needed their help, I seemed so together. Once they knew I really did, things got much better. His family are wonderful but we wasted a year with them thinking we didn't need them and us thinking they weren't really on our side.

We tend to assume friends and family will be on our side, and be helpful to us. The truth is that most of us work to our own agenda. It can be very hard to be truly objective and unselfish. Even people who love you can sometimes give advice, and act in ways that are

!——————————*Task*——————————

We need all the help we can get

Here's an exercise to help you work out how best to use the help family and friends may offer. Make a list of family and friends, such as the one below. Add or remove as fits your situation:

Her parents, sister(s),brother(s)

His parents, sister(s),brother(s)

Her children
His children

Her/his friends

Her work colleagues
His work colleagues

Her ex-partners
His ex-partners

By the name, fill in whether you feel this person helps or hinders you in managing and feeling good about yourself and your new family. When you see, in black and white, who is on your side and who is not, you may be able to make choices. You could do this exercise with someone close to you, either your partner or a friend you trust.   **!**

more in their own interests than yours and indeed are ultimately harmful to you. We tend to adopt an 'all or nothing' approach. This means we feel that if we love them and they love us, we should take the whole package they offer. So if, for instance, a parent hates a new partner or wants nothing to do with children in a new, blended family, we feel torn between them, wanting to satisfy the parent as well as stand by our partner. We want to go on being in contact and we want them to approve but we find doing so can be a strain. The trick to coping is working out your assets using the exercise of making a list.

Once you can see where people fit in, decide whether you might feel able to discuss the situation with each of them, making it clear if you do that you are not accusing them of being unhelpful; you are sharing with them the way you feel about the situation. You might find that people who have seemed unhelpful would far rather be on your side than against you and once you tell them how you feel, would like to change. You may also find they are not willing to do so. It isn't being unreasonable to limit your time with the people who make life hard for you and increase contact with the ones who are pulling with you.

FAMILY FESTIVALS

One of the times you may become particularly aware of problems in a second family is at traditional festivals such as Christmas and Passover and celebrations like weddings, Bar Mitzvahs, christenings and birthdays and during holidays. Events, in other words, which we all particularly associate with families. At the best of times even original families can feel under pressure as all their members expect to be together and to enjoy themselves. Instead of being a time of celebration, traditional festivals may be the cue for the first of many terrible arguments in a second family. Understanding what happens and why can be the beginning of understanding your difficulties and coping with them.

Keeping family traditions alive can assume disproportionate importance in a second family, especially if there are children. You may find yourself insisting on doing something your way, or refusing to do it the way your partner suggests. What is being fought over is not the event itself but what it means to each and every one of you. And what it means, of course, is security and continuity. Families can descend into the most vicious conflict over whether presents are unwrapped singly or in a mad orgy, before, after or during breakfast or who goes to whose house and

!━━━━━━━━━━━ *Task* ━━━━━━━━━━━

Festival brainstorm

Arguments about how, when and where we celebrate festivals and events are usually not about the happening itself but how we feel about ourselves and the other people involved. When you fight because some members want to do it one way and others want to do it another, what is often at stake is a link with the past or the need to feel welcome in or central to a family.

So the key is to ask yourselves; when we disagree about a celebration, what are people asking for and what may they really want?

PEOPLE	WHAT'S ASKED	WHAT'S REALLY WANTED
Her		
Him		
Children		
Her family		
His family		
Her ex		
His ex		
Others		

Brainstorm what you want, and ways of meeting these real needs.   !

when for the celebrations. Finding a compromise that will be accepted by everyone can stretch your ingenuity and you may even be tempted to throw up the whole thing in despair.

When Darren and Joyce had his daughter Sassy to stay over Christmas, they found the three children could not agree.

Joyce's boy Eddo was used to doing Christmas the way she and her first man did it, opening a present on Christmas Eve and then having a stocking in bed and the rest of his presents round the tree with breakfast. I'd always done it the way my parents did, with everything saved up until after breakfast. We did it her way the first few years we were together, when Sassy spent Christmas with her mum. I thought Joyce's way was really good because it spreads it out and means kids don't wake you up too early, begging to have breakfast and begin! Then Sassy came to us one year and all hell broke loose. She kicked up a fuss and said we had to do it her way and no amount of arguing made a difference – she said we were unfair and spoiling things. Eddo said she was the one being a spoilsport and while Earl would have been happy whatever we did, Eddo said he wouldn't change either.

What was really going on here was both children needed to feel secure in their own families. Sassy wanted Darren to celebrate Christmas the way they once did, as if that might bring back the time when she and he lived together with her mum. Eddo also needed to have a reminder of his first family kept alive. When Darren and Joyce were able to work out what the children really wanted and needed, they could all talk about ways these real needs could be met. This left them free to arrange Christmas in a sensible way that suited all of them.

FINAL WORD

Life is a series of processes rather than events. Divorce may happen in a day but the end of a marriage is something that occurs over a period of time – as is the coming together and establishment of a new family. We tend to think marriages end at once, and to expect that a new family should be perfect immediately. We're then surprised and discomforted when we discover it isn't as simple as that and often assume that something is wrong and we're never going to get it right. If there are children in the equation, we may find it particularly difficult, especially if some of them are not related to us. With children you've given birth to you are always undeniably responsible. You can't send them back and you have to like it or lump it. The expectation is that we work hard at finding ways of getting on, not that we should throw in the towel at the first set-back. When you take a child on after their birth, there is always the nagging reminder that you could send them away or walk away yourself. At the back of your mind there may be the thought that you do have a choice and you can say no. Maybe this creates a frame of mind that allows dissatisfaction or criticism, or allows you to imagine an alternative. This may be at the core, or explain the particular intensity, of many of the problems felt by step-parents. Any problem which does arise is often laid at the door of being in a blended family. Normal, natural families do not, we often believe, have all these difficulties, and if only these children were our own everything would be different.

The truth is that no family is perfect and perhaps you need to expect less of yourself and forgive more. Establishing and continuing a blended family is likely to be hard work, but enormously rewarding. You may not realise to what degree any problems that may arise, can be attributed to your emotions and interpretations of what is going on rather than the situation itself. In order to chart a safe and happy course through the possible pitfalls, you need to recognise and explore your own feelings, and those of the other people involved. As an adult you bear the responsibility for what happens in the new family. The onus will be on you to keep trying, but you can only succeed if you understand how and why children react the way they do, and how and why your and their feelings may be different.

PART FOUR
THE CHILD'S VIEW

8

LOSING OUT

We have looked at how and why the adults in a blended family may feel and react the way they do. As you can see, what is going on openly may not be easy to understand or cope with unless you've examined the complex and often mixed feelings under the surface. This is not only true for the adults concerned, it is also true for the children. Children have thoughts, responses and emotions that are every bit as strong and complicated as ours. The problem is that they often find it even harder than we do to understand or deal with their feelings and may hide them better than we do, too. On top of that, children may find it particularly hard to talk to anyone about their concerns or confusions over the break-up of their parents' relationship and the formation of a second family. They may be struggling with conflicting and overwhelming emotions but be unable to share them with you, especially if they feel you cannot accept that they have a point of view of their own, and that it will be different from yours. Although you may not have chosen to break up with your original relationship, you make the choices about the new one. Children, however, have no power at all over the ending or starting of their parents' relationships. The only power they have is to show their dissatisfaction.

They can do this with a frightening effectiveness but frequently with very little control or insight into how they really feel and what they are doing. When faced with what a child may be doing around the time of a change in family status – and this may begin before you publicly admit to a break or long after the new family has come about – parents often want and ask for help with their behaviour. Children may become sullen and argumentative, have tantrums or become depressed. A common reaction is to return to conduct more suited to a much younger child, and to become whiney and clingy, disobedient and rude or to go back to wetting the bed or soiling pants. Their conduct is often seen as inexplicable, especially as the child may well be unable to tell you why they are doing this and you may not feel it is connected with what is happening in your love-life. Concentrating on stopping the behaviour rather than trying to understand *why* a child soils or won't listen or be disciplined will be doomed to failure. If your blended family is to be a happy one, and if you are to help the children involved, you will need to understand how they are feeling and why. In a blended family you are going to have to accept possibly difficult and uncomfortable conditions. One of these is that you are going to have to take into account the views and needs of the children.

TAKING THE PLACE

Adults often think that because they have a new partner, this person should replace the missing parent in the child's life, too. Our emotional needs may best be met by drawing a line under the old relationship and starting again with the new one, and perhaps even pretending the old one never existed. This will be totally at odds with what the child needs. Bella, now 56, has never forgotten the shock she felt when her parent's marriage finally ended when she was five and she was introduced to her father's new wife.

When I was brought to where my father was living, I met again a woman I knew previously as my father's secretary. 'Oh, hello, Jane,' I said. 'You mustn't call me Jane any more,' she replied. 'I'm your new mummy and you should call me mummy from now on.' I asked what had happened to my mummy and was told I mustn't mention her again, and certainly not in the presence of my father,

as she had been extremely wicked and it upset my father to have
her mentioned. It is simply amazing how the ramifications of what
happened over 50 years ago still linger on, and reverberate through
all our lives. Whenever my step-mother introduces me to an
acquaintance as 'my daughter', I feel a wave of anger sweep
through me, as it reminds me of the secret that was maintained to
all those 'not in the know' during my childhood, that I was their
child. This was not done to make me feel good, but to cover up the
'scandal' of my father's divorce.

Kuki lost her mother when she was seven. She remembers her
father coming to fetch her from her grandparents, saying, 'Your
mummy's died but you're going to have a new mummy.' Her
parents had been close friends with another couple, the husband
of which had died three years previously. They were neighbours
and the woman had been helping while Kuki's mother was ill.
Kuki's father thought what he said would be reassuring and
comforting to his daughter and it seemed to work, in that Kuki
never cried in front of him, never talked about her dead mother
and was quiet and obedient. As she grew older, however, she and
her step-mother fought, she was cold and distant with her father
and her own first marriage ended in divorce. When Kuki and her
second husband sought help from a counsellor, she soon realised
that she had never really come to terms with not only losing her
own mother but having her replaced in this way. Both Bella
and Kuki suffered from low self-esteem, the result of feeling
abandoned by their own mothers and of being brought up by
women who had their own reasons for needing to undermine their
husband's daughters.

As adults and parents, we frequently make decisions we
think are best for our children, because the result seems right. An
example would be delaying telling your children you are breaking
up to give them one last Christmas or Passover together as a
family. You may feel this is the correct move, because they
apparently have fun and are happy. Barry remembers his parents

taking him and his sister on a last family holiday without telling them they were divorcing.

The first we kids knew about it was coming home from holiday to find a 'For Sale' sign up outside our house. We were stunned and all I can remember about the rest of the day was arguments and tears as my parents tried to unpack and we ran about begging them to tell us what was happening. Until I started having counselling, I've hated going on holiday. I always had this feeling of impending doom. I could never relax and enjoy, I was sure something awful was going to happen. I've also never trusted my parents since that day. I mean, they lied to us and fooled us and that hurt. And, in fact, the one thing we never told them was that we had a sense that it was coming anyway. They thought the holiday was a great success but for that sense of something about to happen. We both, my sister and I, had it on the holiday. We knew, so the only result was not to give us a good time but to make us think we had to try hard to please them, and then we felt we'd failed.

Barry had coped with his pain at his parent's split by distancing himself from uncomfortable emotions. When he and his partner Jean set up home together, he maintained a cool aloofness from her children Steve and Tracy. He was neither cruel nor unkind but simply remote and while he could accept, in theory, that this was a reaction to his own situation, he was quite unwilling at first to explore further. He had spent so many years holding feelings at arms' length it seemed that the possible benefits of untangling the knots of why he and the family were having difficulties were outweighed for him by the pain of facing up to his past.

Children often believe they're to blame
for the ending of their parents' relationship.

Children take the ending of their parents' relationship very personally. Hardly any relationships break up because one or other of the partners decides that they no longer want to be a parent. They break up because the two adults find they can no longer sustain their relationship with each other. But children don't see it that way. The husband and wife relationship is not one they consider to be your most important role. You're there to be their mum and dad, and instead of realising that what has happened is that being husband and wife is longer satisfying, they see it as mum or dad has got tired of them. While you may be struggling with feelings of failure because you are wondering whose fault it was that your adult relationship broke down, the child is doing exactly the same thing wondering what they did to lose mum's or dad's love.

When a new partner comes along, all of these fears and worries may be directed by the child against this adult. The child may want to gather up all their feelings of anger and bitterness and heap them on the outsider. They may also want to test this new person. If the natural parent, who owes them more allegiance and love than a stranger, can turn their back and walk away, won't this person be even more likely to give up when the going is rough? The child, feeling rejected and abandoned, may want to test to destruction the new partnership to see if the new adult will also decide the child is unworthy and unlovable and give up on them.

FEELING POWERLESS

By and large children do not like being in a blended family. In their eyes, they have little or nothing to gain by co-operating. Children are obviously able to see when you are happy or miserable, but are less able to understand what causes those emotions and of what relevance is their behaviour. The child may feel guilty or bad, or even responsible for their own misery and perhaps yours. But at the same time they don't really believe that their being co-operative or obstructive could have any effect on the new relationship. Asking them to welcome a new partner because they make *you* happy simply does not wash with them. Their own emotional reaction will overwhelm them and this will say the new person is an intruder. The child has no say in the breakdown of the original relationship, and there is no compromise offered on this, as far as he or she is concerned. Yet, in the new family, compromise is likely to be the first thing the child is asked for. So why should the child co-operate or even understand what is being asked of him or her? One way of giving young people more of a sense of involvement and control is to listen to their views in a round-table discussion.

Adults often use 'family discussions' as a way of telling children what they have decided to do. It isn't, however, a true family round table unless you listen as much, if not more, than you talk and unless young people are given as much opportunity to have their say as are adults. Round-table talks may not always be what you need. There will be plenty of times when simply having the time and space to talk with and listen to someone else in the family is important. Try to make a point of allowing every member of the family some time simply to be respectfully heard by you and by the other adults. Both the new partners and the ex-partners need the opportunity simply to share information and feelings as time goes on. But it's a good technique to try if you are having problems and need to clear the air and one that, if used regularly, can head off disagreements. A set-piece round-the-table discussion between everyone concerned in the new set-up may be the best way to start off a blended family. If you feel that children are too young to give their views, or that you are uncomfortable about listening to them, this may be a difficult exercise for you to become accustomed to. It may seem false or awkward to think about sitting round a table actually explaining your views or listening to someone else's, but however silly all this sounds the fact is that it can be enormously helpful. If you find that a discussion like this gets you nowhere or ends in argument, you might consider asking for help in getting it going

! ========================= *Task* =========================

Family round table

Kick off a family round-table discussion by 'brainstorming'. Brainstorming is when you say anything you want to say, within some guidelines. These are the same as those for constructive argument that are outlined in chapter 2. The most important rule is that everyone has to 'own' what they say. That means, you have to begin what you say with 'I think' or 'I feel'. No one can say, 'So-and-so says', or 'Everyone knows', or talk about what other people do or what you think they think. You can talk about how other people's behaviour affects you, by saying, 'When you do such-and-such, I feel . . .' but the aim is to put your point of view, not to criticise or attack other people. Remember, the key is to confront problems, not people. You might start by going round the table letting each person say one thing. Some families have a 'facilitator', who ensures that everyone takes it in turns to speak without interruption. If you do this, let everyone, from oldest to youngest, have a turn at being facilitator. Or, use an object to point out whose turn it is to speak and ask everyone only to talk when they have had it handed on to them. No one is to be shouted down for what they say. Discuss the points rather than arguing with the person. Set aside time for the discussion and allow everyone a chance to speak, as many times as they like. You can't disagree with what someone says if they are explaining their feelings, however much you dislike or object to what is said or feel it is wrong or unfair. What you can do is say how it makes you feel to hear them say that! Take the opportunity to discuss it, understand why they feel that way, explain your side and see if everyone can come to an understanding.

!

from a counsellor or a conciliator, someone who is trained in helping everyone in a particular situation to have their say and listen to everyone else. You'll find addresses at the end of the book.

WISHFUL THINKING

In the aftermath of a broken relationship, children may appear to be startlingly unrealistic. They may harbour the wish, for an unreasonably long time and against all likelihood, that their parents will be reunited at some time in the future. Their hopes for a reunion can sometimes be translated into direct action. Children are perfectly capable of deciding to see off a parent's partner and to wreck the relationship or marriage. This decision would not be made out of malice or cruelty, but because the child would genuinely believe they were doing the right thing both for themselves and for their parents. They will honestly think that if any new mate is removed from the field, the scenario they desire – their parents back together and all the people they love in a happy family again – will come about. Jed, for instance, reluctantly came to the conclusion that his two children Tom and Jesse had deliberately set out to sabotage his relationship with Jan.

It took me a long time to accept that they were doing it deliberately but I have to admit, that's the way it looks. It struck home one weekend when there was a film on TV, an old one with Hayley Mills playing twins who bring their parents back together again. The kids were watching it and I saw this moment when a knowing look was passed between them and then they looked at me. It hit me, good God, they think after all this time if Jan was only gone, all they'd have to do is wangle it and I'd get back with their mother. I told them life isn't like that, but I could see they didn't believe me.

EARLY PROBLEMS

Problems can start with a child during or immediately after the break-up of the original relationship. The child can be truly awful to the parent who is left holding the fort. Tantrums, depression and accusations for having caused the break-up or driven away the errant parent are common. The child will often add insult to injury by insisting that the leaving parent is some sort of saint and has to be treated with kid gloves. This can be immensely painful for the parent looking after the child full-time, particularly if they feel that it's the other parent who properly should bear the brunt of any anger, if he or she is the one who decided to leave. This is a further example of seeing it from the adult point of view, not the child's. The child has pain, anger and fear that has to be given expression somewhere. They child dare not focus this on the parent who has left for fear that he or she will withdraw even more. After all, hasn't he or she already proved that he or she can and will leave if the going gets tough? So the only person the child can target is the parent who stays. The parent with whom they live full-time is the one they vent their pain and anger on, because he or she will have to stand and take it. At the same time, this unfair behaviour can be a deliberate test, even if the child doesn't realise it. The fact that one parent has gone brings the horrible suspicion that the other might go too. So in trying your patience to the limits, the child is testing to see if you too will throw up your hands and walk away.

Children in blended families often feel torn between their separating parents. It may be difficult for an adult to remember that although you have probably only known your ex-partner for part of your life and may no longer feel any obligation towards them, the child has known this adult all their life. Both parents are fixed points in their landscape and the loss of one can be earth-shattering. The child will want to maintain as much contact as he or she can and will feel intensely disloyal if asked to turn his or her back on the missing parent. Children will not take kindly to one natural parent running down the other. You may have perfectly good reasons for being angry with the other parent and to feel that they deserve your criticism, but the child will regard criticism as being directed against themselves as well. Whatever has happened or is happening in your relationship, the child will feel continuing loyalty to both their mother and their father. Hard as it may be for you to acknowledge, a person can leave much to be desired as a partner and still be a good parent. Even though you may feel they do not fulfil their role as father or mother, children have standards and needs that differ or are separate from ours and they are likely to feel a bond and need to continue contact even if the adult does not.

Children are rarely 'better off' without the missing parent. I often receive letters to my magazine agony page from parents who believe their children would be far happier if all contact with the other parent were to be stopped. Common complaints are moodiness and depression immediately before and after a visit, outbursts of temper and bad behaviour. Adults may also claim that the other parent is unreliable or mistreats children and cannot be trusted with them. In spite of all this, children are likely to want to go on seeing the missing parent. However badly they may have suffered, and may still be suffering, the child will still feel a connection, if not love, and a need for contact. A bad reaction to visits may be more because they pick up your expectations that it should be stressful or unpleasant than because that is how they experience the event. And, of course, children may react miserably because the visit is too short rather than that it happens at all. Visits, after all, only serve to underline that parents live separately and it will be the fact that they can only see their parent in this artificial way they object to, not to seeing them. Most of the time, young people who act up around visits do so because it becomes the time when all their confusion, bitterness, anxieties and feelings of loss come to a head. A parent may feel that cutting off contact improves matters, by stopping the sulks and tears. In reality, it merely transforms the sadness from being something that emerges and is focused on specific occasions – the visit – to something that is hidden and continual.

A PARENT IS FOR LIFE

The love of a partner for a partner may die, but the link between parent and child, however mixed up or difficult, is for life. To you, 'parent' is the person who looks after the child and is consistently there for him or her as well as providing food, clean clothes, a nice home and earning the money to make this possible. When another adult takes over responsibility for these details, you may feel that he or she deserves to be given the regard, respect and status due to and of a parent. But to the child, 'parent' is an identity. Even when that person no longer takes care of the day-to-day details, they are still their parent. To the child's understanding, being a parent has more to do with their own identity than the parent's role. If the one who has left ceases to be a parent, a part of the child's own identity will be lost. Paul asked his father, when he was nine years old, whether fatherhood was something that changes, as marital status does:

He'd obviously been worrying about this and he suddenly asked James, 'If Mum gets married, will you still be my father?' James told him he'd always be his father, that doesn't change just because parents remarry. Which, of course, isn't true for everyone because I think he asked the question having seen friends' fathers disappear after divorce. So he wasn't only talking about Laura, he was talking about us, too. This was one of the reasons we haven't married, because we got the impression that Paul would be less secure if we did.

The new partner can be particularly resented if either of the adults tries to paint the absent parent as 'bad'. Even if by anyone's standards this may be true, you'll need to understand how this strikes the child. Since part of their own identity comes from that parent, accepting the parent who is no longer there as wicked, and the time they spent together as a mistake, is the same as having to accept that they themselves are partly wicked and partly a mistake. Whether it is asked for, earned or justified, a parent will have unquestioning loyalty invested in them by their own child and even when a child rejects a parent, they will reserve their greatest anger, disgust and blame for themselves as somehow having caused or deserved the abandonment.

Alternatively, children may take the side of the parent with whom they stay. They may refuse all contact, saying that the abandoning parent has let them down and deserves to be rejected. The full-time parent may find this reassuring, as if being chosen by the child justifies your position, especially if you believe you have not forced their decision. Sadly, young people often don't need to be told openly what you want them to do – they will be able to work it out for themselves. They may choose sides, not because they really don't love the one who has gone but to placate the one left. But you will be sadly mistaken if you think that this allows them to make a fresh start. Losing touch with a parent can lead to enormous inner conflict and a loss of self-worth in a young person that can have lasting effects into their adulthood.

BEING SINGLED OUT

The child may be ashamed of being 'different' and so not want to reveal the change in circumstances at home, or if this itself is no secret, of their own reactions. Darren's daughter Sassy lives with her own mother, coming to stay with Darren and his second wife Joyce, her son Eddo and their son Earl. Darren says:

She hates kissy stuff on stations. If I go to pick her up for the weekend, she'll just walk up to me and go on walking as if we've just been together two minutes before. She's the same if I drop her off, she'll get on the train and never look back or wave or say goodbye. When we're at home, or even out as a family, she's one of those people who's forever flinging her arms around you and kissing and hugging. But saying hello and goodbye at stations – I think she feels that's the sort of thing only kids who don't live with their family do. She probably thinks it singles her out as a part-timer, so she won't do it and show the world she doesn't live with us.

Children may come to accept family break-up and appreciate the blended family and new step-relations, but for an awful lot of children it is a stressful and difficult arrangement about which they have very few choices. Even if the adults concerned are making the transition quite easily, the tug of loyalty in the child may cause enormous conflict within them. A central fact for children in a blended family is that loss of some form or other must always be involved. They lose out in so many obvious ways. For a start, they will have lost one parent and the sense of being in a secure family. They will have experienced a loss of innocence. In this context, innocence has nothing to do with sexuality but is connected with a comfortable feeling that all is right with the world because dad and mum love you and will always be there. After any loss there can be feelings of guilt, anger, remorse and mourning. The child may well believe that something they did, or failed to do, led to their parent leaving, and feel inadequate and unlovable. They may ask, 'If I'm good, will Dad come back?' and if he doesn't, be convinced it must be because they have been bad. The lost person will probably be idolised. However badly they may have treated their partner or even their children, once gone the child is likely to feel they can do no wrong. And since this 'wonderful person' has abandoned them, their own sense of value and self worth will be damaged.

_____ SIGNS OF STRESS _____

Children in blended families often revert to babyish, disruptive behaviour that you might have thought they had grown out of. Whatever their age they may revert to bedwetting or having temper tantrums, or to clinging, whining behaviour that demands attention. Disruptive behaviour can often be divided into two broad areas – harm to others, where the anger and confusion is being turned against the outside world, and harm to themselves, when it is turned inwards. Examples of the first could be bullying at school and vandalism. Examples of the second could be truanting from school, doing badly at work or, in slightly older children, sleeping around, drug-taking or joyriding. Some children may even turn to self-mutilation, cutting themselves or having tattoos put on. In early adult years there can be hasty, early marriage, often followed by divorce. Girls from blended families often express a desire to marry early, believing that they can win back the happy, intact family by recreating it in their own. Boys often say they intend not to marry at all or not to have children of their own. There may be a dramatic contrast in the way they behave inside and outside the home. Some children show their unhappiness by difficult behaviour only at home and act perfectly normally at school or with other relatives and friends. Some turn it completely around and appear perfectly normal when they are with you but raise hell in school or outside, often to the total surprise and astonishment of their parents when the whistle is blown. Difficulties can be further complicated by the fact that the young person will often not tell anyone outside the family what is happening, let alone what they feel about what is happening. This can obviously lead to problems if outsiders, such as teachers, make unfair judgements on what they see as unexplained and unreasonable moodiness and lack of concentration, or miss the significance of pointers to disturbed behaviour.

Just as adults come to a new relationship with all the baggage of unfinished business from the past, so too do young people. Joyce's first partner was an alcoholic and abusive to her and their son Eddo. He left when the boy was three. Darren moved in with them a year later and neither could understand why Eddo, who formed a loving and affectionate relationship with his new step-father, would sometimes throw tantrums, run to his room and cry. They eventually realised it was when Joyce and he were drinking cans of beer, although not when they opened a bottle of wine. Darren didn't drink to the same level as Eddo's father or get drunk, but the opening of a can of beer was enough to cause such anxiety in the child that he was beside himself. Similarly, children may react to any cue that brings back bad memories from the past, just as adults do, without realising the trigger.

But disturbed behaviour is not so much a reaction to separation and new family patterns in themselves, as a symptom of not understanding how to deal with the resulting loss and conflict. However strange, destructive or odd their behaviour, what they are doing is trying to cope with unhappiness and confusion. In fact, adults practise similar coping techniques when faced with these emotions. The only difference is that we often don't expect to find them in the young because we think they don't understand and therefore don't notice what is going on, or because we're indulging in the wishful thinking of, 'If they're quiet, it must be all right'. We hope they will trust us to be on top of the situation, and take apparent acceptance to be a sign that they are. Young people are particularly adept at putting on an 'It doesn't matter – I don't care' facade. Being 'cool' is important to many teenagers, but refusing to show feelings is more than an adolescent pose. In fact, what young people of all ages often do is try to cope with their fears or griefs by burying them and avoiding thinking about, talking about and facing up to emotions about a split or a new relationship. As well as avoidance, young people may deny there is any problem and steadfastly maintain all is well, even when their misery is noticeable. In addition to denial, they are likely to withdraw, becoming silent and non-communicative. Sadness may be firmly repressed, so the child may appear to be in a good mood, but suffer from tell-tale physical symptoms such as headaches, stomach pains and general ill-health. Children, as well as adults, can also project their feelings, where they externalise or cast out their uncomfortable thoughts on to someone else. The sort of overwhelming, painful feelings so many children will be having at this time can be too much for them to deal with. Instead of being able to say they are angry with the missing parent, they'll want to get rid of these feelings and transfer them to someone (if not everyone) else, rather than that they have them for the people they also love. Hence the impassioned 'You hate me, everyone hates me!' of many an unhappy young person.

RETAINING THE LINKS

The bottom line in all this is that children have a right to retain workable links with both their birth parents just as much as the parent has a right to a new partner. Which means that compromise, with adults getting what they need and children getting what they need, is what has to be worked towards. The most important fact of all to recognise is that children are separate people, not merely an extension of their parents. They have their own desires but often they need your help in achieving them. Both parents and children can want and need something that is not only different but may be conflicting. Rather than one of you getting what you want and the other one losing out, the trick is to identify what these different things are and then to negotiate towards a position where both can be satisfied. For a start, it may be difficult understanding and accepting what sort of contact a child may be able to deal with. Children up to the age of three have a very strong attachment to the person who looks after them most of the time. This doesn't have to be their mother but can be the father or grandparent, relative or other carer, whoever holds them, feeds them and is most familiar to them. A child would find leaving this carer for any length of time stressful, so any form of contact that means nights away or even a whole day with the parent wanting access would be unwise. A parent seeking contact may feel they are being prevented from getting to know their child properly but the truth is that having visits at the child's home, in familiar surroundings and with the main carer there, is best.

Once a child is three years old, they can leave their primary carer to spend a whole day with a known and trusted adult or stay over. Weekend visits, however, may start and end in tears or the child may be frightened and sulky. This is because visits a week apart are too distant. After as short a time as a day, a child loses touch and begins to feel the adult has gone for good. Each time they go and then reappear, the child feels anxious and upset. Daily contact, with the adult dropping by to put the child to bed or share an evening meal, as well as having the child to stay or taking them out, is what they need. Children may also be able to keep in touch with regular phone calls and by sending and receiving letters, cards or notes to maintain the link between them and a parent they don't see every day.

From the ages of five to 12, children are able to deal with weekly contact but it must be regular. Structure is important to children and knowing when and where the parent will see them, and having these fulfilled, is really important. Although parents will need to make the arrangements, children should be consulted and involved in what is to be planned. This is because once they start school, they develop friendships and may have other things they want to do as well at weekends.

From the age of 12, young people can and should make their own arrangements, and should feel able to call or call round as often and when it suits them and the parent they want to see.

!════════════════ *Task* ════════════════

What do we want?

This is another 'brainstorming' exercise. Sit down with your children round a table. Ask someone to do the writing and give them a large sheet of paper and a pen or pencil. Divide the sheet into four columns, with these headings:

What do the adults want?
What do the young people want?
What helps?
What hinders?

Make a list of all the things you want and all the changes each of you would like to see. These may range from, 'I'd like the kids to tidy their rooms', or 'I want to be able to use the phone when I want', to 'I want us to be a proper family', to 'I want to see Dad whenever I like'. When you look at the list, you may find some of your and the young people's 'wants' are quite unrealistic or actually seem to work against each other. For instance, if you had said you 'wanted to be a proper family', you may have meant 'I want my ex to leave us alone'. You can't have your wish if the children's is to have frequent contact. Discuss how conflicting wishes help or hinder each other and fill in the next two columns. Discuss what you all want, and why, and talk over how and why the items you've put in the other columns operate.

   The next stage is to use this knowledge and understanding to find a realistic solution. Choose one item you all feel is important. Looking at all four columns, decide what it is, what helps and what hinders. Discuss what you can all do to decrease the hindrance and increase the help. Then, do it! Once you have found a way with one item, work your way through the others.

!

_____SPECIAL PROBLEM?_____

Children in blended families often find that the very place they might have expected to receive support, only adds to their discomfort. Alex remembers that his primary school teachers were less than helpful:

An awful lot of people of my age had parents who were separated, remarried and so on, so it wasn't as if I was the only one. But a great deal of my time at school seemed to be spent explaining to everyone that, for example, my father and mother probably won't or can't attend parents' evening together because they live separate lives. And when Suzie came to a parents' evening too, I was stumped for how to explain who she was, mainly because everyone asking the question seemed nonplussed as to who she could be and why she was there. I mean, what is the word for it? Your step-mother (but they weren't married at that time so that wasn't right), your father's partner (not a description they understood), his girlfriend (that's not exactly the best term for anyone over the age of 18, really)? Step-family relationships are difficult at the best of times and you spend a lot of time trying to find new rules and definitions of what's what. This process is very important to those involved because thrashing it out is what makes it work. The last thing you need is people who cannot deal with what is now a very common phenomenon or who try to put a name to it for you, without listening to what you want to call it.

Teachers daily encounter the reality of reconstituted families. A recent study in one class of nine-year-olds found that 79 per cent were no longer living with both their parents full-time. Most teachers are sensitive to the fact that not every child has two parents living with them. But there seems to be little official recognition and little training to understand the complex dynamics of two-parent families where one of the adults may not be related directly to the child in question, or one-parent families where not only the non-custodial father but his new partner are also keenly involved in the upbringing and well-being of the child. It may be understandable that schools and the teachers working in them would be unprepared or caught off guard when faced with the complications of a blended family. What is less forgivable is when, as so frequently happens, official ignorance is converted into open pressure, which upsets children and thus puts pressure on the relationship. Alex found that some of the teachers in his school were not prepared to take on board his happy acceptance of his situation:

'Not Suzie,' a teacher once said to me at Junior school, 'Auntie Suzie'. As if, not being my real mother or my father's real wife, I wasn't expected to be on first-name terms with her. Which was particularly stupid considering that I call both my parents by their first names half the time, anyway!

Do the children in a blended family really present a special problem? Problems experienced by children in a restructured family are often thought to be the inevitable result of the situation. Arguments between adults and children tend to be typed as being all about step-family conflict rather than due to normal adult/child conflict. When everything else is equal there seems to be little real difference between those in original families, and children in a blended family. They are not found to be any more troublesome or troubled or achieve less at school. However, there may be a temptation for the adults concerned to make the nature of the family a focus or even an excuse for any and all dissatisfaction or miseries. All children argue with their parents and all children can be sullen, graceless and rebellious at times, and especially during the teenage years. Most of it isn't personal, and it's certainly not to do with being in a blended family. The danger with feeling it is all about blended families is that we can become fatalistic and complacent. After all, we say, if what is happening is inevitable, there's nothing we can do about it, is there? The truth is that it's not family breakdown or second families that cause the trouble but how we deal with it. If young people from second families have a poor record of achievement and are more likely to leave school, marry early or suffer their own marriage breakdown than children who stay in their family of origin, the reason is likely to be how their feelings about family changes were dealt with rather than with the changes themselves. Adults in a second family often have lower aspirations for the children involved. This may be because stresses and tensions in the home mean that you want to give them an easy time and make little demands on them in their school life. In some cases, adults want the children they live with out of their lives as soon as possible and so encourage them to leave school and enter employment quickly. Some children may welcome a liberal 'hands-off' policy that lets them drop out of school or college or demands little in the way of work achievements. They may be resistant to facing up to and dealing with their sadness, grief and anger but, in the long run, we have a responsibility to help them to do so.

We must remember that a young person who behaves in a manner you find unpleasant may not be a 'bad' child, but one who is trying to say something to you. In contrast, a 'good' child, who is quiet, controlled and obedient, may not be acting in a normal, healthy way at all but be hiding their feelings. Naughtiness and being awkward at least show energy, creativeness, curiosity and *life*. And 'bad' behaviour may only be so in the eyes of the beholder. You may want to label something the child does or says as wicked, not because it is actually wrong, but because it may unwittingly touch a sore point in you. An adult who is new to a young person may have a misunderstanding with them and believe the child has disobeyed deliberately when in fact they haven't yet learnt or understood the new adult's rules. And sometimes what appears to be naughty or rude behaviour is simply a reasonable response to a dreadfully sad situation. If you believed, absolutely, that one of the two people who meant most to you had decided you were a waste of time and deserted you and the other had installed a new love in your place, wouldn't you be tempted to pull the hair or kick the shins of the interloper? So why be surprised when your child takes against a step-parent or step sibling?

If one child out of several children reacts badly,
don't assume the child is the problem
rather than the situation.

Just because only one child out of several children reacts badly, don't think this means the child is the problem rather than the situation. Children are likely to react in different ways depending on their age, their gender, their position in the family and what has happened to them up to now. A very young child, for instance, may accept a new adult as part of their lives with little comment. They may, however, suffer hidden worries about why their parent has gone and be left with lingering fears that it was their fault. This can emerge later in life as a lack of self-esteem and self-worth. The age of the child at the time of the break-up and when the parent's new partner appears also has a bearing on how they cope. Paul's father's partner Deirdre came along six years after his parents separated.

She hasn't been around from when I was too young to remember, but certainly long enough for it to feel it's always been like this. I think that I was lucky that my parents split up when I was one, before I knew what was going on. Not only did I miss out on any unpleasantness or upset surrounding the actual separation, but I've also only really known my father alone or with Deirdre. I think that if I'd had to sit and watch James and my mother at the split I might have had a rather more confused attitude about his relationship with Deirdre. The same would have been true if Deirdre had been part of a long line of girlfriends.

The relative age of the step-parent and child can also affect how well the child and new adult get on. When Kerry met George on holiday, it was actually his 12-year-old daughter she first got to know and she has always made creative use of the fact that she is nearer to his children's ages than she is to his.

We were both early morning swimmers in the hotel pool. On the second morning, she and her two brothers were playing pool volleyball and somehow I joined in. I'm only 10 years older than Adele and I've no dignity whatsoever and we all mucked about and had great fun. She told her dad to invite me to join them for breakfast, I stayed with them for the rest of the day and the rest, as they say, is history. But the point is that I've always acted towards Adele and the two boys more like an older sister than a substitute mum. I'll play with them and when I do act my age and ask them to do something, it's still more like an older friend than a parent. Being closer to them in age than their mother had meant they've never seen me as someone trying to take her place, which is fortunate.

The time that has passed between a parent withdrawing from a child's life and a new adult arriving can also have a great effect on how the child will welcome any newcomer. In some families, a parent and child, or children, build up a special and close relationship, in the other adult's absence. This can develop even while the original couple are together, if one adult spends much of their time elsewhere. This may simply be a case of a child enjoying the undivided attention of the parent, with special games, private jokes and a lot of time spent together. In other circumstances the child can be leaned on quite heavily by the adult for emotional or practical support. The child may then take on what amounts to adult or even parental responsibilities. When a new partner comes along the parent may be aware that the child is missing out when their attention and time are given more to the new partner than to the child, but think the child would be relieved at having responsibilities beyond their years once more lifted off their shoulders. In fact, children often resent being replaced, and the new adult not only becomes in their eyes a substitute and a rival for the missing parent but for them, too. Jean found this the case when, having had four years on her own with her daughter Tracy and son Steve, she met Barry.

What I really hadn't realised until it was far too late was how much I'd relied on them both. And how much they'd resent Barry for taking their place. I blame my mother in one way, because when my first husband left me, she told Steve, who was only 10 at the time, that he'd have to be the man of the family and look after us all, and of course poor Steve took this very seriously. And I suppose I confided in Tracy far too much and far too early. So when Barry came along and moved in, Steve saw him as a rival and the two of them were always scrapping. And Tracy felt left out, because she and I didn't talk the way we did before. I thought at the time I was doing them a favour by not burdening them any more.

SIBLING HOSTILITY

Rivalry may emerge in a blended family from other quarters. As well as adjusting to a new adult in their parents' and their own lives, young people often have to adjust to new children, living with them, visiting or existing in the background. And, if and when children are born to the new couple, there may be more half-brothers and half-sisters and further step-children. Whatever the complexities of who lives where, another loss felt by any or all of these young people may be of their own position in the family. A young person who was once an only child may suddenly acquire older or younger siblings. Someone secure and settled in their role as oldest child or baby of the family may feel pushed off their throne by another child. Even when there is no ill-feeling between the children themselves, there may be extreme unease at the new arrangement, with anger and resentment directed to the adults. Often, however, there may come jealousy, bullying and even violence and abuse among the young people. Children may be convinced their parents now prefer another child to them and they may resort to attention-seeking behaviour to reclaim their rightful place. In all these cases, each child may find him or herself with shifting, complex feelings of jealousy and guilt. A child may be jealous of children who seem to be occupying as much time and attention, or even more, than the child does in their own birth parent's eyes. And there may be feelings of guilt if they themselves have taken a central role in the life of the new step-parent and they can see the step-parent's birth child losing out.

SEXUAL AWARENESS AND EMBARRASSMENT

A child or young person can't help feeling left out as a parent carries on a love affair with the new partner. Young people of whatever age find sex intriguing, fascinating and exciting but look upon the idea of parents having sex lives as hilarious, ridiculous or downright disgusting. By the time children in a family of their birth origin are old enough to ask questions about and be aware of sexual activity, it will usually be a settled, comfortable exchange which goes on between parents without children consciously noticing. In a blended family, sex and sexuality may be all too visible and this can cause difficulties. The child may express his or her unease and revulsion at adults 'carrying on'. Children may feel driven to compete with their own parents, either by having their own sexual relationships, or by flirting with the parent's partner, if of the opposite sex, or a step-brother or step-sister if there is one. The child may also flirt with the missing parent, either as a way of keeping and not losing them too, or as a way of competing with the parent who has failed to do so. While open sexual behaviour is obviously more likely to be the route taken by teenagers, it can appear in even younger children. Tragically, this can often lead to premature sexual activity, and unwanted or unplanned pregnancy.

SEXUAL ABUSE

The fact that some of the people involved in a blended family have no blood relationship can lead to deeper, darker and more troubling difficulties. Studies show that step-fathers are five times more likely to abuse children sexually than natural fathers. The reasons for this may be many, varied and complex, but one element could be that the fact that the child is not their own simply removes one further taboo against doing it. Other men or boys in the family may also find it possible to sexually abuse a child more easily if the child is under their nominal authority because they may be considered to be a brother, an uncle or a grandfather, but know they have no blood-linked connection to the child. Particularly worrying is that sexually abusive adults do not act out of the blue or suddenly. Their behaviour is not prompted by the child in question but by their own emotional and sexual needs, which often date back to their own childhood. This means that abusive men may actively seek out women who have children, with access to the child as the real incentive for pursuing the relationship. However much you love a new partner and however much you may suspect a child has reasons for wanting to drive a wedge between you, it may be vitally important to listen to and trust a young person who tells you that a new adult is harming them. Children may find it hard to put this into words. They may be feeling guilty and confused, and child abusers are particularly skilled and experienced at manipulating their victims. The signs may be depression, moodiness, ill-health and isolation. If there is the slightest suspicion, ask for professional support and help, from your own doctor or from one of the professional organisations listed in appendix 2.

Sexual abuse also affords the one exception to the rule that contact between parent and child is always vital. When there is any risk that a child could come to physical or emotional harm through being with a relative or anyone they might know, there is good reason to alert the authorities. Sadly, this does mean that some angry parents are prepared to 'play the abuse card', by using a false accusation of sexual abuse as a means of preventing an adult from seeing their child. Since the person who suffers the most damage from this would be the child, it is never justifiable.

Children may not only be at risk from adults, however. New siblings may offer danger, too. Children may not only resent a new parent in their lives but also be jealous and angry about the trespass into their lives and their home of other children. A subtle pecking order tends to be established in a family as children grow up together. There is plenty of evidence to suggest that birth order – whether you are the eldest, middle or youngest – and whether your siblings are the same or the opposite sex to you, has a great bearing on the position in a family each child takes. The sudden arrival of step siblings may overturn this entirely, so a favoured only or oldest child may suddenly find themselves with an older brother or sister. The youngest child, used to being the baby of the family, may suddenly have to take a back seat as little children arrive to take their place. This can lead to anger that might be shown in bullying and even in other forms of abuse, including sexual abuse. Sometimes step-children may be mutually attracted to each other, with no intention of coercion or abuse. The problem they encounter, however, is that there may be enormous hostility towards the idea of any relationship between them, because they are considered to be related even when they are not. A strong friendship that could give them support and help may be prevented by the rest of the family, because the adults involved feel that their feelings for each other are somehow wrong.

Heightened awareness of the lack of boundaries between

adults and children in a step-family can also lead to other forms of difficulty. Parents may find it hard to talk to their children about sexual matters, even about the most basic sex education, for fear of somehow stepping over an invisible and shifting line. The very fact that one or both parents may be openly conducting a sexual relationship at a time in their lives where sex may otherwise have faded into the background can cause other problems. Teenage children, particularly girls, may become sexually active far earlier than they might otherwise have chosen to do. Alternatively, they may fall back into behaviour young for their years, finding the idea of dating and showing an interest in the opposite sex so frightening and disgusting that they avoid friendships with the opposite sex.

LIKING NEW FAMILY MEMBERS

If the new adult turns out to be someone the child can and does like, the situation may become even more difficult. The young person's confused feelings can make it even harder for them to accept the new partner and they may add guilt at their own disloyalty, as they see it, to the mix. The nicer the new partner is, the more torn a young person may feel. The more they find themselves drawn to and liking the replacement for their own parent, the angrier and more hostile they may become. The child can feel guilty at allowing the new parent to take the place of the old, and so be angry with him or herself, and also be angry with the new partner and the other parent, on behalf of the mum or dad who is being replaced. The child may actually start to act out a parent's role, by leaving home or refusing to have contact with one parent or by making demands that seem out of place. In effect, they are playing the divorcing or divorced role to show loyalty to one parent or to punish the other.

NAMES

The imbalance of power between child and parent is often shown by the fact the we call children by their names but they must often call us by our titles – mum and dad. What happens in the blended family is that this way of putting children in their place comes unstuck. Adults are often most unhappy at the idea of children calling someone older than they are by a first name. This unease is often explained by saying it sounds rude or cheeky, as if the child was claiming a status, that of equal or friend, that we think they shouldn't have. Strange, isn't it, that we feel uneasy at the idea of children claiming the intimacy of friendship or equality with the very people with whom they should have the closest possible relationship?

Faced with their parent's partner in a new relationship, a child is most unlikely to want to call them dad or mum, for all the reasons of resentment, jealousy and guilt that we have already discussed. They may even wish to signal the reassessment of their relationships with their own birth parents by calling them by their first names, too. Children in blended families are quite likely to give some thought to this whole question of who you are, who they are and, as signified by these names and titles, what your relationship to each other is. Their conclusions may actually in some ways make for the possibility of a better relationship but can cause discomfort to their parents because nothing is taken for granted. Paul feels that in some ways his relationship with his father is not the same as it would have been if they had lived together.

My father and I are similar in character in that neither of us is good at showing or admitting to feelings. We are not as close or in contact as much as we would like, because neither of us is likely to ring the other and suggest getting together very often. It tends to be Dree or my mother who make the suggestion. This has a lot to do with what I feel about him as a father. I sometimes feel that he's more a friend than a 'significant' relative. This means I'd probably listen to his advice if I asked for it but if he told me to do something I'd be less likely to listen than if my mother had told or asked me to do the same. I like visiting him as a friend but at the times in my life when he's been trying to guide or push me, I've quite often wanted to stay away. This is because when he gives me strong advice or criticism, I don't think our level of contact gives him the right, and when I do, I then feel I'm being short-changed and he's 'failing' me as a parent. But the upside is that I know from my own friends that when we do talk it's with more depth than most fathers and sons do. I get a lot from my dad and I don't think it would have been like this if he'd lived with us.

Which surname a child goes by may also become very important. The child may want to change their name if, for instance, they are living with a remarried mother and a step-father and do not want to be singled out as odd in having a different name from them. Alternatively, a child may cling against all the odds to a name conspicuously different from that of the rest of the family as a way of retaining a link with the missing birth parent. Some children even choose to change their first names as a way of keeping a missing or dead parent alive. Adele, George's daughter, was actually known by her first name until the age of 13, when she decided to adopt her second name, which had been her mother's as well.

Kerry has always been 'dead cool' about letting us call her by her first name and never insisted on being 'mum', unlike the step-mothers from hell some of my friends have. She was the one to persuade my dad that I wasn't being silly when I said I was Adele from now on and she's never called me by my old name, not once.

George had not realised the import of his daughter's decision and what lay behind it until he mentioned it to a counsellor. He had felt she was just being a 'flighty teenager' (as he put it), picking up trendy ideas and making choices one day that would be discarded the next. Once he had understood why she was making this request, he stopped teasing her and tried hard to do what she wanted. But he also needed to understand, and discuss with his daughter, how he felt about using his dead wife's name once again.

! ————————— *Task* —————————

Making a life story book

Children like stories. It helps them make sense of the world and their place in it. When a small child asks you, 'Where do babies come from?' they're really asking where did they come from, how did they get there and where do they belong. When a family changes, we often shy away from exploring the whys and wherefores with the young people involved. Not only do we then, also, often stop talking about what is happening in the present, we frequently draw a veil over the past. This leaves children feeling insecure and cut off from their roots. Forgetting or ceasing to talk about an ex-partner and our life with them may help us but it hurts our children. A valuable exercise for them, and us, is to invite our children to create a Life Story Book. Using photos and pictures, old cards or letters, memories of their own and stories from you, help them to chart their own life, from birth to now, with all the high and low points, the triumphs and sadnesses. Give them the option to do this on their own and to keep it private, or to share it with you and others in the family.

!

9

WICKED STEP-PARENTS – WHAT THE MYTHS MEAN

The myth of the wicked step-parent is one that most children have heard and may readily embrace when they find themselves entering a blended family. It's worth understanding that this myth actually has nothing to do with step-mothers, step-fathers or step-brothers and step-sisters at all. These myths have come about as a coping technique to allow children to make sense of their new situations and reactions to their own parents.

As they grow, children discover that the loving, caring mother can also be the punitive, angry mother. When children first experience emotions, they find they can love all-embracingly, but also hate equally powerfully. These feelings are over-whelming and the child needs to find a way of dealing with them. Before a young child can integrate these opposite sides of him or herself and the parent, and accept they can exist side by side, they 'solve' the paradox by projecting all the bad aspects elsewhere. So, when a story tells of the saintly mother who dies and is replaced by the wicked step-mother, this in fact is a reflection of what the child feels happens when loving mother disappears and is replaced by angry mother. Eventually the child grows up to a point where he or she can recognise that someone can be angry with you and go on loving you at the same time, and that you can do the same thing.

> The myth of the wicked step-family is actually a technique
> to help developing children to cope with mixed feelings
> about the people they love.

This separation of different parts of yourself and of your parents
is a very valuable part of development. We need these devices to
give us time to understand ourselves and our feelings. A problem
arises, however, when we get stuck with them. All of us have to
struggle with and come to terms with this 'splitting' of ourselves
and others into good and bad. As we grow up, we learn to accept
and mix the good feelings we have with the bad ones. We learn
that we can be angry and loving towards the same person. We
learn that people can do nice and nasty things, or things that
please as well as things that upset us and that this is acceptable
and normal. Getting stuck means you go on, like a small child,
feeling that it's all or nothing – all good or all bad with no shades
of grey. When this happens, you may feel your parents or your
partner can do no wrong, and you can do no right. Or that the
children you have taken on can do no right and neither can their
other parent. The danger lies, in effect, in taking the 'wicked step-
parent' myth literally. When the story is swallowed hook, line and
sinker by children and adults and used to project their anger,
grief or confusion over the death of a relationship or the
beginning of a new one, it does not help anyone to resolve
uncomfortable feelings. Instead, it prolongs them. It's far more
comfortable to feel that you don't harbour nasty, destructive
feelings for another person, but that they are monsters who are
somehow responsible for all the bad things that are happening.

   In fact, all young people harbour the fantasy of not being
their parents' real child at some time during childhood, especially
in adolescence. If they are feeling alienated from the rest of the
family or angry with someone inside it, it's quite normal to
indulge in a daydream about being the foundling child of a rich or

royal family who one day will reclaim you and take you away. Just as with the step-family myth, it's a way of coming to terms with the fact that you may hate and be angry with the people responsible for you at the same time as loving them deeply. For children in a blended family, however, the fantasy has come true. While in an original family a child has to come to terms with their mixed feelings, a child in a blended family may never have to reconcile their anger or disagreements with the adult in authority with the recognition that the adult does love them. In an original family a child eventually gets over their anger. In a blended family, it may remain with them and form a permanent barrier.

These feelings are not by any means confined to the children concerned. In recent years there has been a rash of popular films and books that portray children as possessed or evil. These are really the other side of the wicked step-mother myth, and they can reassure angry and confused adults that they may be right to consider the troublesome child as a deliberate and conscious schemer. Don't assume this, or you and the child can both get off on the wrong foot. You would see a deliberate campaign or entrenched attitudes when there are none, and also condemn the child as 'knowing' and 'bad' when the fact is that he or she is simply as confused as you are.

A CHIP OFF THE OLD BLOCK?

Adults watch their own children develop and often, without realising it themselves, adjust and adapt themselves to this development. So when an already formed step-child comes along, the average adult is uneasy. This child cannot be moulded in the same way as any of their own, and indeed will often react against any attempt at such moulding. Frequently, a child displays characteristics it inherits or copies from the other parent and this can become a bone of contention. The child may find it immensely comforting to know he or she does something 'just like your dad/mum', whereas the new partner may find it irritating or a painful, living reminder of the previous relationship. Adults may feel considerable repressed anger towards an ex-partner which the child may feel is directed against him or her. This may either be because you only sound off in front of the child, or because in railing against their parent, they feel implicated too, or because you *do* get angry with the child, when something in them reminds you of their other parent. It's very important to recognise what it is that makes you upset and to be honest and direct with both yourself and the child concerned.

Many difficulties between child and adult are caused by adult/child dynamics. We don't respect children as people or listen to their views very often. If we could recognise that they are individuals, not just little copies of ourselves, we would all be better off. If one adult tried to control another in the way that even the most permissive of parents controls their children they would very soon find themselves being labelled as bullies. We hit children, and call it smacking rather than assault. We pull them behind us to the shops, and tell them off if they protest. What often happens when a step-parent comes on the scene is that children, probably quite rightly, take the opportunity to revolt and say, 'You have absolutely no right to assume this kind of control over me.'

CHILDREN UNDERSTAND MORE THAN WE THINK

It is often tempting to assume that a child is too young to understand what is going on, or to take on board the complexities of adult emotions. Even at quite a young age, young people are also able to make reasoned judgements on adult relationships. In fact, even very young children can often be extremely perceptive.

They are sometimes even more perceptive than adults because they have not yet learned to dissemble or forgotten how to tell the truth. Where an adult may be fooled, perhaps because they want to accept the polite fictions of the white lie, a child may see straight through any evasion. Children can often also be quite refreshing in that they can be direct about their feelings and let you know in no uncertain terms what they think, if you are prepared to listen. 'In-your-face' arguments can be better and easier to deal with than adult veiled insults and behind-your-back plotting! The major difference between child and adult, however, is that children will persistently see any problem basically from

! ───────────── *Task* ─────────────

Drawing up a contract

If you've practised Family Round Table and What Do We Want?, you may find you all could do with a clear way of keeping track of what you want changed and how you've agreed to go about it. One way of doing that is drawing up a contract.

The idea is to write down exactly what everyone has promised to do. The key is that it shouldn't be one-sided, with one person or a few people asked to make an effort or make changes and other people acting as usual. Work out a fair exchange and one you can all agree. Make a precise record, including:

What you've all agreed to do
How you agree to do it
When you agree to do it by and for how long

Everyone should sign the contract. Review it regularly and if the terms are not being met, discuss why and whether the contract needs to be redrawn or something needs to be adjusted.

!

their own point of view. An adult may be put off explaining why a marriage is breaking up because the child's apparently naive solution is that everyone can still go on living together. But it's not really that the child can't understand, it's that they don't necessarily want to understand. The child needs both of you, the child loves both of you so why on earth can't you go on living together? As far as their needs are concerned, that is neither a silly question nor a ridiculous solution. It's very easy to forget that adults know from long experience that however difficult your present life may be, things may improve. Children have only the recent past and the present to go by and these may both be distressing. You have to put yourself in their shoes in order to understand what they need. Perhaps the most important key to doing this is to listen to what the child says rather than steamrollering them and constructing what you would *like* them to have said.

WHAT MONEY MEANS TO CHILDREN

Money may be tight in a blended family, particularly if one of the adults concerned is also having to maintain or contribute to two households or there is only one, or no, wage-earner in a family. Just as adults use money, deliberately or without realising it, to make a point in a continuing argument, children may do, too. Young people of all ages these days are very aware of market forces and spending power is important to them. A tight budget may be a source of shame and discomfort to a young person in any family, but when their family is a new one they may feel that lack of cash draws attention to their state, and is all the fault of your being in that situation. They may continue to ask for items you cannot afford and get angry or even abusive when you refuse. You may feel they are being stupid in not taking in your explanations as to why money is short no matter how many times you spell them out, which misses the point.

The continued requests are their way of registering their complaint, not about the lack of money but the loss of the original family. Because of their highly emotional state, children themselves may encourage conflict, between you and your ex-partner, between their parents and new partners and between you and them. Money is commonly used in families to play out disputes about other things. This is why it can become a focus for children who need to find a place to make their anger and anxieties heard. Many take advantage of a lack of communication to play parents off against each other, or try to turn parent against step-parent. Some children in a blended family may be encouraged by others in the same position or themselves realise the opportunities for emotional blackmail. The familiar cry of 'But Mum lets me stay up late', or 'Dad says he'll buy it for me' may often be used by the child to get extra privileges or treats. It's very easy to find yourselves competing with each other in this way but what the child gains is always a substitute for what it really wants, which is attention and proof of love.

While young people may ask for money as a way of asking for love and attention, they similarly may refuse, damage or misuse things bought for them as a way of rejecting overtures. Robbie's grandchildren have mixed feelings about his second wife Janet, mainly because their mother has found it very hard to accept the death of her mother and the re-marriage of her father. Janet makes an effort with them so they play with and talk to her when she visits and their mother is polite. But, especially at Christmas, the children seem to take a special delight in either breaking or ignoring the presents Janet gives them. While all the adults continue to pretend to be friends, the children show what is really going on under the surface. They also hide when Robbie asks them to 'Kiss Granny Janet' or give in with bad grace and then make a great display of wiping their faces.

THE SPACE AVAILABLE

Whether or not members of a blended family seem to get on, any
new arrangement means a lot of changes in a household which
can be very unsettling for all involved. Where a blended family
sets up home can be terribly important. Whether the parent and
children move in with the new partner or the new partner joins
what had been the former family home, or whether all move in to
a fresh house can affect what happens next. For adults, having a
new partner move in or going to join them in another home could
well be an exciting and welcome beginning. Many adults might
expect the children to share this thrill too, but the chances are
they will not. A step-parent moving in can find him or herself
resented by the children involved who will see the newcomer as
an invader. In any case, this adult may not feel truly at home, if
the home had been shared by someone else before them. Children
could be particularly uneasy and alienated in surroundings they
feel are not theirs.

How you divide up living space in your home will have
considerable bearing on what is happening at a time when
relationships are in the fragile early stages. The move may result
in crowding if the family cannot afford the size of home the
household now needs and everyone has to cram themselves into
too small a space. Children who have previously had their own
rooms may have to share. This can cause enormous resentment,
especially if two sets of children are being blended who resent
being forced to live side by side with step-siblings. The privacy
and security of your own room can be a haven at a time when the
privacy and security of what you had thought was your family is
being burst asunder. So it can cause particular anxiety when this
retreat is removed. Human beings, just like any other animals,
have very strong feelings about their territory. A child may feel
that the house is no longer theirs and they don't belong. They
may feel robbed of privacy or of status and that other members of
the family have been unfairly given better conditions and more

consideration than they have. Even the joy of getting a new house or treats that have been long promised – space to have a pet, a room of their own or a garden – may be overshadowed by the loss of familiar surroundings and having to share the house with people they haven't chosen to live with.

While a totally fresh start would seem to be the ideal compromise, children need the comfort of familiar surroundings and resent being uprooted. The child may want to retain that last link with the missing parent, or the missing life that may be seen as idyllically happy 'until you spoiled it'. A new home may also mean that children lose touch with friends and neighbours, who may have become particularly important at a time of instability and insecurity. They may equally 'lose' friends even if you do not move house, if the new arrangements mean that they feel too ashamed or shy to bring their friends home any more.

The space available for children who visit on weekends or for holidays can also be an important factor in the success or otherwise of the new family. Cramming in to a small space may also affect your ability to be like a 'normal' family, especially if this crush only happens on occasions, such as weekends when the children come to stay. Deirdre, who has lived with James for 18 years, remembers with regret the way they handled contact with his son when he was younger.

We made a stupid mistake when we bought our first place together. It was a one-bedroomed flat near the city centre. If we had had any sense, we would have got two bedrooms, but James thought it was silly spending money we couldn't afford, or having to live further out than we wanted, for the sake of having a room for Paul's occasional visits. Big mistake. He may not have stayed a lot, but when he did it just rubbed it in that he didn't have a place in our lives but slept in a put-up bed. He didn't have a stake in our lives, so it seemed. Every time he came, he'd walk around checking up that everything he remembered was still there. And because the place was small, we would always be going out on treats. That wasn't right. What he wanted, and we really needed, was just to slop around and be together as a family. We would go out and he would get tired and bored and frustrated. And we would feel panicky that money was short, and get annoyed that he wasn't grateful for the treats. We would bicker, that would terrify him and things would get fraught. In our new house, we have two spare rooms and we've given him a key. As far as I'm concerned, he has a room here and can come and go as he pleases. Of course it's a bit bloody late, and I wish we'd done this 15 years ago.

However much the children may be welcomed in a new home or a new relationship and however much they may otherwise have liked any newcomer, establishing a new home is likely to lead to tension. Children may bristle like a pack of cats and be unable to come to terms with hostile and aggressive emotions. These reactions are likely to be strong enough when just another adult is involved; when you combine children of different parents, they are even stronger. One tip is to use a family round table to discuss the situation, perhaps reallocating the bedrooms of everyone in the house, so at least you all have a new room to be starting off with. The defence of your own territory is such a basic instinct, even with the very young, that you have to make allowances for and understand these feelings. If you don't already have the rule in your household that children have a right to privacy in their own space and that even adults should ask permission and knock before entering, you may find it helpful to introduce this now.

Living arrangements will make an enormous difference to the success of a new extended family. Studies have shown that when parents have split up and a child is dividing time between them, their well-being will be dramatically increased if the two households are within walking or cycling distance. This means that the child can choose when and if to see the other parent and indeed can 'pop round' at times other than those formally arranged. If this isn't possible, it is at least essential that they can feel that they have a place in both households. If the available space is not enough for them to have their own room, they should at least have a corner that they can think of as theirs where belongings can be safely left until their next visit.

A divided lifestyle can put confusing strains on young people. Continuity and consistency are very important to them and it can be difficult enough within a family when parents who live together have different ideas and different styles in their personal attitudes and the way they approach child-rearing. But this confusion is obviously increased when parents live apart, especially if there are other adults and maybe another family involved. But the old idea that a child's need for stability means they must have one and only one home may not be true. Children who feel they have a proper base in both parents' homes are more likely to survive the experience of divorce or separation and a new blended family than those who feel they have no place in the leaving parent's life.

ROUTINES AND SCHEDULES

One problem that comes up again and again is different styles or standards in upbringing in different families. This often results in the step-child resenting the position held by the new step-parent. Sometimes the statement, 'You can't tell me what to do because you aren't my real mother/father' is a heartfelt howl of protest at losing their birth parent rather than a show of defiance. Feelings of loyalty and love for the missing parent make it very difficult for the child to offer anything but hostility towards the new adult in their life. But sometimes awkward behaviour is a genuine reaction to confusion over demands that are simply not understood. We all have our own expectations, rules and beliefs and what you consider the right way to behave may be totally foreign to a child new to your routines. You can create problems for yourselves by going to extremes, either by insisting that the new family conforms exactly to the routines and traditions that you or they have known before, or that, symbolic of the change, everything must be different.

Routines and schedules can give a vital stability to children. Young people tend to challenge rules all the time, objecting to bed times, to having to tidy their rooms or sit at table to eat meals. It's easy to get the impression that they'd happily welcome a life where 'anything goes'. Nothing could be further from the truth. Young people push against the boundaries in order to find out where they stand firm. They want and need structure in their lives and if, when they push, the boundaries keep giving way, rather than welcoming this it can make them feel anxious and frightened. After a period of disruption children may find it difficult to return to having routines and fixed schedules and you may find they object if you try to establish these. Alternatively, you may find children – especially visiting, part-time children – insist on a set programme or pattern. Long after you would like a bit of variety, they may be clinging to the familiar and known. Children may ask for the same bedtime story, the same evening meal, the same, unvarying, day out. Routines give an enormous measure of security, so discussing them with everyone involved and both establishing and maintaining them are important.

Even children who have enjoyed a more flexible and bohemian lifestyle may react to the strains of a restructured family by wanting something more 'ordinary' and even boring, a demand which can be extremely irritating to their parents! Continuity is very reassuring to children. If you are combining two families, the chances are that there may be differences in the way you run your households. This can often lead to distress to the children involved. So often with these unhappy situations, you may find yourself in a 'no-win' situation. If the new adult makes an effort to adopt the child's familiar routines and schedules as if they were theirs too, the child may become resentful as if the adult were cheating or being a phoney. Then again, if you don't lay down rules and let the children get away with not doing chores, you won't really be doing anyone a favour. They won't know where they stand and you may build up a store of resentment.

Some step-parents, in an effort to endear themselves, slip into the pattern of being too nice, making every effort to give the child their favourite foods and not demanding that they do chores. This is particularly prevalent in weekend step-families where children only visit for a limited time. The problem with this behaviour is that it only emphasises the fact that the children are visitors and that the situation is unusual. Children and adults really need to feel that this is a normal, usual relationship, and the only way to do that is for everyone to behave as normal. This includes being able to make demands and occasionally blow your stack. Otherwise, you will simply build up resentments that will expand out of all proportion. By all means spare the rod, but don't shy away from natural confrontations with a step-child.

If children only visit you or stay occasionally, it can be particularly easy to fall into the Treat Trap. Food has a special symbolic place in our society. We offer food as a proof of love, and eat it sometimes to comfort or reward ourselves. We often also reject food as a way of punishing ourselves or the person giving it. It has a very powerful role in all families and particularly families with any sort of problem. Because their visit is a limited and eagerly anticipated occasion, you may want to mark it with a relaxation of the usual demands and to celebrate. Unfortunately, this only serves to underline the out-of-the-ordinary nature of your relationship. It puts unfair pressure on the child, and on the other parent. Deirdre and James only saw his son Paul at weekends or during his school holidays, when either or both of them would take leave from work. Deirdre would make a point of filling up the fridge with his favourite drinks, cooking the foods he requested and taking him out to special events:

Paul said to me a couple of times that he wished he lived with us full-time and I know Laura used to get quite exasperated at the little brat going home and going on for hours about the wonderful time he'd had. I had the sense, one time, to point out to him that if he did live with us it would be very different and just like living at home. After that visit, I tried to act a little less special, like telling him to get his own drinks from the fridge when he wanted one rather than getting them for him. When he comes to visit now, we hardly ever go out. We just slob around, watching television or reading the papers and chatting – just like a real family! We all have a far better time and if I have just one piece of advice to give to other people in our situation, it's not to make visits any different from just any normal family day.

What can often be difficult for parents is not realising that their children do have their own private lives which are perfectly separate from the parents' lives. Something that is important to you is of no significance to them and vice versa. Something that is welcomed by you can be a tragedy to them, and vice versa. You may thus find yourself thoroughly confused sometimes when your child is simply not seeing an event in the same light as you

---

! ───────────── *Task* ─────────────

Household chores – who does what?

Even children who come to stay occasionally or irregularly should help around their part-time home, and have chores to do, if it is to be a home and not a hotel. However much they may object to doing work, they will in fact be getting the reassuring message that they belong and have a stake in what is a home to them. Of course, the principle is that everyone does their share, according to their abilities.

Get a sheet of paper and pens and brainstorm, with every member of your family, which chores need to be done. Draw up a schedule of daily, weekly and occasional tasks. Ask everyone to agree to taking turns, or taking on chores as theirs. Draw up a contract and review it regularly.   **!**

are. For instance, you and your new partner may be eagerly anticipating and planning an anniversary that is special to you, and be totally puzzled at the child's ill temper that spoils an otherwise happy day. But from the child's point of view you may just be rubbing salt into the wound, if they see the new partnership as nothing to celebrate. Similarly, there may be an anniversary that is important to the child – such as the day they first realised their birth parents were splitting up – of which you are entirely ignorant. On, or approaching, that day you may be at a loss to understand why the child is so unhappy. Days that you think ought to be happy ones, such as birthdays or Christmas, may in fact be extremely painful if the child wants to be with both their parents and this is not possible.

DIFFERENT VALUES

The day-to-day workings of a blended family can produce many difficulties for the young people concerned. Step-parent and step-child might have radically different values. Natural parent and child can clash, but this is not because you have different beliefs. After all, children do get most of their value systems from their own parents. Most disagreements are really about independence and responsibility and are a way for children, even those of a very young age, to assert their right to stand on their own two feet. When the dust settles, more children share more beliefs and ideas with their parents than have strong differences. However, in a blended family, adult and child can certainly have a very different set of values and even young children may be surprisingly independent about these. Added to the importance of defending your values to prove you can rebel against your parents – something all children have to do – may be the importance of defending yourself and therefore the missing parent against a take-over by the new partner. As a blended family sorts out a mutually acceptable way of getting along, this harmony and agreement may in itself cause problems. The missing adult may feel their child is growing away from them and accuse the other parent and the new adult of 'poisoning the child against me'. The reality may be no more than the child becoming accustomed to living with different ideas and standards, but any differences can be felt as a deliberate affront by one parent. This can lead to noisy and entrenched arguments about very unimportant things. The argument that is raging, needless to say, is hardly ever actually about the specific item that is being contested. There are all sorts of things we say or do that have a deeper and wider meaning. Our actions are often

! ================= *Task* =================

Giving the same message

A major difficulty in blended families is the variety of mixed messages young people may feel they are getting from the adults around them. Separated parents may agree, openly, to a set of standards – such as not spoiling children with treats, insisting they don't smoke and do work hard at school – and then one or both may confuse the children by their actions. Parents may set off with the best of intentions and then find themselves pulling their children in opposite directions, bewildering and upsetting them. It may be important to get clear in your own mind where each of you stands on issues you feel mean a lot and to talk them over. You don't always have to toe the same line, as long as everyone knows you do have different opinions and you're clear how these dovetail or conflict. The key is to agree to disagree and to explain that to your children, rather than undermining each other behind your backs.

Sit down with a large sheet of paper. Down one side, list the issues you want to discuss. Along the top, list the people who may be giving messages. For each person and under each issue, fill in what is said and what comes across. !

symbolic – that is, they stand in for an unstated and often unrecognised communication. The problem is that we frequently misunderstand each other's hidden message. We can find ourselves carrying on a whole 'conversation' without saying a word, and in two or more different languages! It may sound silly to have to explain yourself and to ask children what they mean by doing something, but it could short-cut a surprising number of difficulties.

Children tend to be very accepting of their parents' point of view and less critical of your ideas than you may be of theirs. Most children would like the adults concerned to at least acknowledge that they too often have irrational feelings about what is going on and are not always acting sanely, logically or in the best interests of their children. Alex, my own step-son, feels that his separated parents and myself, as a 'significant other', had petty quarrels over him that were not fully justified:

I think it's very important for everyone involved to understand that it is not just children who have difficulties in accepting a step-family situation. Quite often the continuing relationship of the ex-couple can have a great effect. My own mother and father had periods of the 'your son does this' and 'your son does that' type of behaviour. Not only is this a bloody pain if all you need out of it is a new pair of jeans, but you end up feeling guilty as a result of their disagreement as to what makes up their responsibilities. An argument over whose turn it is to buy new clothes is at the bottom end of the scale, but I suppose that in an extreme situation you could end up actually hating one or both parents for what you feel they are making you responsible for.

MAKE A VIRTUE OF DIFFERENCE

On the positive side, young people can be extraordinarily realistic and even capable of seeing the advantages in being a member of a second family. There are some advantages to the step rather than the natural child/parent relationship. Step-children and parents sometimes know each other better than natural parents and children, because you can approach another person's child as a 'real' person rather than as an extension of yourself. You may find it difficult to love them, but you can respect and ultimately care for and about them. Rather than trying to cover up the differences between original families and blended families, you can celebrate them. Perhaps one advantage of a separated family is that it does almost require parents to make an effort to spend time with their

! ————————————*Task*————————————

In many situations, doing your best for yourself and your child is a case of finding the balance; between what is right for you and right for them; between what they need and what is too much for them to handle. To find that balance sometimes you may have to look carefully at your own behaviour and ask yourself, 'Which side of the line is this?' See how many other items you and your children can pair up and put in these columns. Use this exercise to talk to them about how you can be there for them.

IT'S GOOD TO …	IT'S BAD TO …
Talk to your kids	Tell them inappropriate things
Be interested and ask questions	Interrogate
Be open about your feelings	Show distress so much they feel guilt
Talk about family history	Dwell on the past
Co-parent children	Come between new partners
Acknowledge what you need from kids	Use kids to satisfy your needs
Listen to and involve kids	Ask kids to make choices they can't make

!

! ——————————— *Task* ———————————

Different strokes

Use this exercise to give yourself and the other members of your family a boost. We all need to be rewarded, to be praised and thanked and appreciated. Sometimes we forget how much we need to value others, and to be valued by them. Often, we forget how easy it is to give pleasure and how a little would mean a lot. Counsellors call the sort of action that gives a lift to morale 'a stroke'. Strokes can be spoken – telling someone you love them, thanking them for helping you or saying you value them. Or they can be shown by contact – hugging or kissing someone or giving them a back rub. Or they can be acted out – making them a cup of coffee, giving them a small present or doing a chore you know they'd like done. Make a list of strokes you'd like to give and a list of strokes you'd like to receive and ask the rest of your family to do the same. Discuss them and agree to give each other at least one stroke each today. **!**

children. Parks and museums tend to be full on Sundays with the separated parents and their children having their one day visit together, which could be good for parent and child. It may be worth remembering, however, that while special treats may be welcomed by children, everyday experiences together are actually more important. Most children would welcome the opportunity simply to be with their parent – sitting around their home even if it is an untidy bedsit, and sharing in ordinary chores such as shopping and cooking.

If a blended family is to succeed and children are to accept and be accepted by the adults involved who are not their birth parents, perhaps the first and most important step is for you not to try to conform to any idealised myth of 'the family'. You can't expect a 'happy ever after' to happen immediately. Real life isn't all sweetness and light and there will be conflict and pain, as there is in any family. The most important ingredient is patience. Appreciation, recognition and respect may all come, as may love. But all have to be earned and it is a two-way process. You should be prepared to give everything you would like in return, to make a second family a happy place to be.

PART FIVE
THE SECOND FAMILY IN SOCIETY

10

ARE WE ALONE?

We've already seen that our ideas of what makes up the 'normal' family may be inaccurate. The standard 'two parents + two of their own children' stereotype is a lot less common than you might think. Just look at the figures. As many as one in three people in the UK today are involved in some sort of second family. Even so, the only ideas many of us have of what a step-parent is and what a step-child can expect are half-remembered bits of fairy tales, such as Cinderella and Hansel and Gretel. If the Wicked Queen in Snow White, or the abandoned children in Hansel and Gretel, are the only models you have to go on when imagining what a second family might mean to you, it's hardly surprising that the situation can be a tricky one.

> Most adults and children who enter a 'blended' family
> feel guilty about any difficulties they have,
> cannot discuss their fears
> and feel isolated and alone.

Being in a blended family makes you a member of a very large community. Many people in this community have problems that are unique and particular to them and their situation, but many have difficulties that have as their root the condition they share, of being in a new family group.

We seem to have such a poor view of second families, especially when children are involved, that we have an almost total 'blind spot' when it comes to thinking about them. Sweeping step-families under the carpet interferes with our understanding of what happens in them, even in our recognition of their existence. Even in this digital age, when you might imagine that everyone in the Western world is counted, tabulated and minutely observed, although we can find figures for how many second marriages exist, we don't know for certain how many members of our society are in a step-family today.

The reasons for this rest in the way we gather information about our society. Our main access to information about individuals and families is from a census – a massive exercise where each household is required to fill in a form on one particular, designated night, recording everyone present and some details about them. Up to now the census has not fully explored the precise relationship between children and adults in a household. We can show how many adults there are in this country, how many children and in which households they mainly lived. We can come up with a figure for 'parents and their children'. From records kept and submitted by registrars and other authorities we can find out how many divorces, remarriages and even adoptions happen each year. But all of these, the most accurate figures we can examine about our population, can't always show for certain whether families are related by blood, adoption, second marriage or simply living together.

We can make intelligent *estimates* of how many people have step relationships. Over half of marriages ending in divorce have children, and the number of children involved in the UK is over 200,000. We also know that 50 per cent of divorcees will remarry within five years of the ending of their first marriage. So from this it would appear that around six million people, or about 10 per cent of the UK population, are in a step-relationship at present. But does this give a full picture of how many people are involved in a step-family? Children whose parents were living together but who had never married will not show up in divorce statistics and neither will children whose parents were married but have separated without getting formally divorced. We only count children when their parents divorce, not when they remarry, and we certainly don't have any figures for how many children are involved when a father or mother dies and the surviving parent remarries.

We can make further estimates by doing surveys of representative samples of population groups and applying the findings to the general population. *The General Household Survey 1991* asked a representative sample of both men and women in the UK whether they had any step, adopted or foster children living with them, and found that 8 per cent of families did. *Population Trends*, the quarterly journal of the UK Office for National Statistics for summer 1994, suggests that around 5.5 per cent of all children will become step-children of a married couple and 6.7 per cent, children of a cohabiting couple, at some time before their 16th birthday. Indeed, because couples often live together before getting married, many may be both, several times, before they are through! Comparative findings in the United States suggested 11 per cent of married couples with dependent children are step-families and 16 per cent of all children still living at home have a step-father or mother.

> If you think you are unusual, remember
> one in three marriages is a remarriage for one or
> both partners.

Calculating the numbers of couples who say they have a step-child living with them by no means takes account of many blended families. Even though most researchers consider a stepchild is 'a child of your wife or husband who is not your own', many surveys do not, or cannot, count every child who comes within that definition, and every adult who has a child who does so. The reason we don't know exactly how many people are involved is that we don't all agree what we mean when we say 'step-family'. *Step* in this form comes from the Old English word *steop* which means an orphan. A step-mother or step-father was someone who became the father or mother of an orphan, by marrying the surviving parent. In the summer 1994 issue of *Population Trends*, a step-family was defined as 'married couples, or cohabiting couples, with dependent children living in their family, one or more of whom are not the natural children of both the man and the woman'. So step-families are usually thought to be households made up of a couple with children living full-time, and these are the families counted in research or surveys. The adults caring for them are the step-parents and the children concerned are the step-children.

But in a divided family, the child often has two households that have a link with him or her, and both are equally 'step-family' households. If John and Jane live with their mother Sally, their father Ben's new wife, Jill, is just as much involved in a step-relationship as is Tom, their mother's new husband. Sally is also involved in a step-relationship if Jill or Tom have children from a previous relationship. You are a step-parent if the children

―――――――――― *FACT POINT* ――――――――――

One intriguing fact is that the figure of 8 per cent usually accepted as being the number of families with step-children has hardly changed for some time. The proportion of children who are step-children may not be very different today from a hundred years ago. Yet more marriages are breaking up and more people are having children outside marriage. What may be different is that more women may be deciding not to marry a second time or to live in a permanent relationship when their first has failed. And children who might, 10 or 20 years ago, have been step-children in a second marriage, are now living with one birth parent and a cohabiting partner.

FACT POINT

In almost one fifth of step-families, it is the man who is the father and the woman who is the step-parent. This is a higher figure than you might expect, considering that children usually go with their mother after a marriage breaks up. There are relatively few single families with a father at the helm. This might suggest that men left alone with children are quicker than women to find a new partner to be a helpmeet.

---

involved are seen by you once a week, once a month, some time or never, as much as if they lived with you all the time. So for every 'married couple step-family with resident dependent children' counted in a survey, there must have been *at least* one other 'family' that is also a step-family – that is, the one containing the non-resident parent. And what about families in which children have left home and are no longer 'dependent'? They still suffer the problems of blended families, even if they no longer live at home. In addition, cohabiting couples with or without dependent children may not be counted.

When all the possible variations are considered, the number of people having a step-relationship of some sort may be nearer to 18 million, or almost one in three people in this country. Far from being unusual or freakish, steps are members of a very large group. Very few 'minority' groups can claim to form a third of the population. And if you want to consider how many people are *affected* by step-relationships, it has to be far greater even than 18 million, because step-relationships do not stop at the front door. If you live with or are linked in some way to someone else's children, then your parents, your brothers and sisters, your aunts and uncles, your friends, your neighbours, your colleagues and your employers are affected too. Ask around and you'll find very few people who do not in some way have their life touched by such a relationship, whether it is themselves or someone they know who is actually in this form of second family.

> Step-families take many forms. New partnerships are made after separation, divorce or the death of a spouse or living companion and may or may not be formalised by marriage. One or both partners may have children who may live with the new partnership or remain with the ex-partner, only being seen on certain occasions.

STEP MYTHS – THE WAY WE ARE SEEN

Where do we get our ideas from about families, and also about step-families? Politicians constantly talk about 'family values', shaping and reinforcing the view that family is the source of all stability, morality, security and happiness. So where does that put *step*-families? From Hans Christian Andersen to Dickens, from Shakespeare to present-day films, step-parents and step-siblings are common figures, but they always seem to be shown as the baddies. Even if your parents never told you fairy stories, even if you've never read the classics and prefer soap opera to Shakespeare, you know that the word 'wicked' *always* goes in front of the word 'step-mother' and that step-fathers are supposed to be violent, abusive and sometimes even murderous.

Until you actually become part of a second family you may have felt that these images, these stories, were unimportant. The problem with stereotypes is that they are a part of our culture and they form a background to most of our lives. Having assumptions about people in a particular situation or role can actually affect the way you behave and feel towards them and the way they behave and feel about themselves. Whoever first said, 'Sticks and stones may break my bones but words can never hurt me' was obviously not a member of a second family! Until you make the effort to think about second families and work out why you hold certain views, you may not be able to see the effect the myths have on you.

11

WHAT IS A STEP-FAMILY?

What are some of the assumptions you or the people you know or meet may hold about blended families? The 'wicked step' myth is perhaps the most common and obvious one. Claire's mother died when she was 10 and her father remarried two years later. She found that at least one of her relatives was convinced her father's new wife would be unable to accept or love another woman's child and be would hostile towards her.

I think I was quite excited at first at the idea of having a mum around again. You feel isolated in a family of boys and since it was just me and my three brothers and dad, I was a bit lonely. My younger brother was as keen as I was but the two older ones were unsure. My nan (my mother's mother) kept on about the fact that no woman would want another woman's child. Nan kept telling me to come to her when – not if – she picked on me. And everywhere I looked, it was wicked step-mothers and suchlike. When she came, the whole situation was odd and not at all the way we'd thought it would be. We soon hated her and thought she was against us. I don't think she was but it was as if we all got off on the wrong foot and we couldn't put it right.

Claire herself became part of a step-family when, after a divorce, she remarried Lucas who was also divorced. Both brought children to the relationship and they came for help when it seemed to them that the marriage would fail. In exploring their own pasts, Claire and Lucas both realised that they had assumed a surprising amount about step-relationships. Thinking back to her grandmother, Claire remembered that she seemed to have a double vision of the woman who took her daughter's place. She eventually became friendly and appeared to have 'come round' to accepting her, but still kept fiercely to her views that only genetic relatives could really love each other. Similarly, Claire found herself in despair about her relationships with Lucas' children and his with hers, and fearful of the effects the hostility was having on their marriage, but unsure of how she really felt about them. When she and Lucas sat down to talk about how they felt about 'family', they were able to see how and why they felt the way they did. Over a period of months, they explored their own responses and those of their children and talked far more than they had dared to do about their feelings, fears and needs. After six months of hard work, they were able to say that their relationship and their bond with the children had improved beyond recognition.

The assumption that a new person will find it hard to love children who are not actually their own can put up barriers that are not always easy to tear down. Barry knew Jean had two children by her first marriage when they started going out. He feels no hostility towards Steve and Tracy, although he is aware that they feel angry with him, but his attitude is actually far harder to overcome. He says he is indifferent to them, and views them with a cool detachment. Jean would like to have help in soothing the tensions she feels in their home but Barry is not keen to take part. He says his feelings date from the first time he met her children.

I didn't really think at the time that the fact she had children had any relevance to me. We were just dating and it was fun and the only time I saw them was occasionally when I went round to pick her up and they weren't in bed yet. I took them all to a theme park once and that was really good fun. They liked white-knuckle rides

! ————————————— *Task* ═══════════

Fairy stories

Sit down together and read, out loud, the following opening sections of three fairy stories. Do you know them? If so, see if you can tell each other the rest of these tales. Then talk about when you first heard them and discuss how they may have influenced your ideas about step-families. Can you remember any other fairy tales or myths and legends with a step-family theme? Do any of them present step-parents, step-siblings or step-families in a good light?

1) Once upon a time, a Queen in a distant land longed for a child. Whatever she did and wherever she was, she dreamed of a daughter with skin as white as snow, lips red as blood, and hair black as ebony. After years of waiting, she fell pregnant and to her joy a daughter was born – a girl the image of her dreams. The King was just as happy as she and they called the girl Snow White. But before the child reached her second birthday, the Queen died. The King mourned the wife he loved but within a year, he married again. The new Queen was beautiful, but proud and jealous. She had a magic looking glass, and when she stood in front of it and said, 'Looking glass, looking glass on the wall, who is the fairest of them all?' the glass would answer, 'You, oh Queen, are the fairest of them all.' But when her step-daughter reached the age of 14, the day came when it said, 'You are the fairest here at hand, but Snow White is fairest in all the land.' And from that day on the Queen schemed to do away with her step-daughter.

2) Once upon a time, there was a merchant who had a beautiful, kind wife and a lovely daughter. The daughter was barely 12 years old when her mother died and after a year her father married again a woman with two daughters of her own. They were fair of face but black of heart, with tempers to match, and very soon the house rang with their demands. Quarrels and heartache filled the home until they drove the merchant's own daughter out of their sight. They treated her like a servant and soon she took refuge in the kitchen and became a scullery maid. They took away her fine clothes, her silks and satins and forced her to sleep by the fire in the kitchen, in the ashes. Because from that time she always had streaks from the cinders on her face and in her hair, they called her Cinderella.

3) Once upon a time, a woodcutter lived in a great forest with his two children. Their mother had died when they were young and as they grew older, he had taken a second wife. When the children were 12 and 14, their luck took a turn for the worse and they became so poor that their clothes were rags and they had very little to eat. One night the wife took her husband aside and said, 'Tomorrow I want you to take the children into the forest until they are lost and leave them there.' Their father was horrified and refused but she insisted. 'We can feed and clothe the two of us, but unless we get rid of the children we shall all starve.' When she said that, the woodcutter sadly nodded his head and said he would do it. But Hansel and Gretel overheard their step-mother talking and set about making a plan to save themselves.

as much as I do and Jean is a wussy about rollercoasters so we were having our own fun together. It was when I moved in that the trouble started. I want us to have our own children and Jean thinks she – or as she puts it, we – have enough. But they're not my kids. They're not bad kids and I'm happy they live here but I can't get involved or worked up about them. Sometimes that's a good thing as I can deal with any problems they have in a dispassionate way, not getting worked up, like the time Stevie was caught nicking sweets and Jean went ballistic but I took it calmly. But the bottom line is that they're not my own blood. How can you be expected to love children who are not your own?

LOVING CHILDREN NOT YOUR OWN

Well, why should it be so difficult to love someone who is not genetically related to you? After all, we do it all the time, in that the strongest and closest emotional link in our lives will be with someone who is a genetic stranger – that is, our partner. There is, however, a difference. Whether we accept or realise it or not, relationships are never as selfless as we believe. All are, at core, conducted in 'I'll scratch your back only if you scratch mine' terms. There is always a form of return, even if you do not immediately understand it. The pay-off for committing yourself to a non-related partner is, of course, the pleasure and delights of a loving and sexual relationship. The reward of having children is the unconditional love found in the bond between children and their birth parents and the fact that your immortality is assured by furthering your own genetic blueprint. None of this is available when you bring up children who are not your own. Since human beings, just like other members of the animal kingdom, are programmed to see anyone different as an alien, an invader and even an enemy, it is this programming that may be causing problems in your blended family.

> We're programmed to see non-relatives
> as the enemy.

Hostility to a child who does not bear your own genes is very natural. Any living being, whether human or other type of animal, is driven to try to preserve and further its own genes – the blueprint that is taken from your cells and repeated in your own offspring. If you look at animals that might seem to resemble us most, you can see that caring for your own is a 'survival trait', a way of behaving that maximises your chances of living and furthering your genes. Animals that live in large groups and give birth to one or two young at a time, such as antelopes or cows, act in much the same way as we do about our own children. They're protective, exclusive and when push comes to shove, survival of their own often involves throwing someone else's to the wolves, because the instinctive programming is designed to achieve survival of the species as a whole and sometimes this is gained at the expense of individual members. If the herd is surrounded by predators, fit animals will make a run for it, leaving the sick and the lame as bait so they can get away safely. Offering help to an orphaned or abandoned youngster would put your own offspring at risk, so no one does it. And this is so deeply ingrained that even if their own offspring die, they will still reject someone else's. Any farmer can tell you, when trying to foster a young calf or lamb, the only way this can be done is for the foster mother to be fooled into believing the youngster is her own, by tying the animals up together until the baby smells of the new mother or by wrapping a newborn lamb in the skin of one that has died. So, it would seem that having no parental feeling for a child who doesn't have a genetic link to you is something that we cannot hope to change.

But the animal world offers variations of social behaviour beyond caring for one's own offspring to the exclusion of all others. Many animals are not exclusive and share childcare.

Wolves, wild dogs and meerkats have crêches, where one or two members of the pack will baby-sit all the youngsters as the other adults go out to hunt. Lionesses will suckle any hungry cub in their pride, whether they are their own or those of a sister lioness. Admittedly, members of these groups are often related and it could be argued that by looking after your sister's or your cousin's child you further your genes as much as by looking after your own. But it shows that in Nature not all animals require children to be strictly their own before they will parent them.

What humans have in addition to our 'animal' nature is the ability to think and act on more than instinct. We now talk about the 'global village' and are coming to see that the whole world is

! ——————————— *Task* ———————————

Family brainstorm

Start this brainstorming session by using the guidelines already outlined on page 151.

Here is a list of words and phrases to describe families and family life. Get a pen and sit down with your partner. Add any words that come to mind. Don't, at this stage, discuss the words that either of you suggest – put them all down without any comment or disagreement, however strange they may seem to either of you at first.

Security	Sadness
Warmth	Happiness
Arguments	Resentment
Jealousy	Depression
Rival	Protection
Love	Risk
Envy	Confidence
Acceptance	Reassurance
Rejection	Help

Fulfilment	Attention
Memories	Care
Future	Advice
Past	Children
Company	Husband
Loneliness	Wife
Peace Stress	Pets
Tension	Holidays
Traditions	Trust
Ordinary	Patience
Different	Talking
Obligations	Making time
Support	Listening
Loyalty	Being there
Absent	Sharing
Betrayal	Managing disappointment
Togetherness	

Take a large piece of paper and divide it into three columns. Label one column 'Ideal', one 'My childhood' and the third 'Our family'. Put the words under the heading you think they apply to (words can be repeated in two or three columns), and go on adding any other words that come to mind. When you've run out of words, look at which words you've put under which heading. Talk about the words that you have used. Why did they come to mind? Why do they belong where you've put them?

Now, take a fresh sheet and divide it in two. Label one side 'First family' and the other 'Second family' (or third, or wherever you are now) and repeat the whole exercise.

really one extended community. Is it too much to expect us also to see that the inhabitants are nothing more or less than an extended family? Parents aren't always good, kind, loving, selfless and caring to the children they give birth to, so 'natural instinct' fails to protect children in some situations. Conversely, it may be just as natural to care for children not born to you with exactly the same love and protection you might offer your own. What is interesting and significant is what helps you to do that, and what stops you. The myths, of what is and what isn't a family, often get in the way.

SHARED TRAITS

When someone says they cannot feel a kinship with a child or an adult because they are not a blood relative, what is often being expressed is the importance of sharing traits. When we look at a person with whom we have a blood link, we see physical similarities and treasure them, as a reminder of our bond. But we also respond to habits and behaviour that are picked up, over the years. These are not inborn, even though we think they pass down only by inheritance, but learned, which means that you can

! ———————————————— *Task* ————————————————

Family trees

Creating a family tree can have a number of useful functions in a blended family. It can help children to retain their sense of connection to birth relatives, even when they see them less often than they would like. It can help adults to accept and acknowledge that these links are important to their children even when they themselves no longer wish to maintain the connection. It can help children and adults to see how the family has altered but that it is still a family, albeit a different one. It can help all the members of the second family to make bonds and build a new structure. Rather than trying to pretend you are 'a normal family', try to make a virtue of the diversity and spread of contacts. In many communities, both in the past and in the present, people live in larger groups than we do. There are advantages in this. After all, when you have two parents living together with their children there may be times when everyone has their own concerns and cannot spare time for others. When you have 'a new extended family', there is more likely to be somebody free to listen or to be there for you.

Get a large sheet of paper. Sit down with the whole family and, starting in the centre of the sheet and using the following symbols, draw your own family tree. You could use photographs and drawings to illustrate each branch of your tree.

Woman

Man

Married couple

Unmarried couple

Separated couple

Divorced couple

Children of couple

Adopted and fostered children

Person who has died

Date of marriage

Date of divorce

Age at present and age at death.

acquire them from or give them to people who are not 'your own'. My step-son, for instance, has a passion for science fiction and fantasy novels, graphic novels and films with special effects. Neither his mother nor his father can stand them, but I've been a fan since before I knew him. It might be a coincidence, but it's more than likely that he learned this taste from me. Even though you and members of your second family may not share an origin, you can still see how you are likely to form links that can bring you together and mean as much as a blood bond. One way we confirm a shared family history is to talk about it, passing on stories about the things we or relatives have done. Another way is to look at photographs or portraits, which show the near or distant past. Second families often become awkward about doing this, because they feel as if they are drawing attention to a part of the family that doesn't 'belong' to another part. New members may feel at a disadvantage and fear comparisons and old members may think stirring up the past will only make them depressed. Far from underlining loss or creating resentment, thinking and talking about the past can only be helpful. If you try to pretend nothing existed before your present family structure you live a lie which makes it difficult to develop a future form. Far better to use photos, stories and even a family tree to show how the past still lives, but has transformed into the family you now have.

KIDS COME TOO

Myths about what is and isn't a 'normal' family can make it difficult for your second family to bond together. More specific myths about step-families themselves can be even more unhelpful. The 'wicked step' myth often hinders blended families who are trying to form relationships that will work for them. Another myth that can intrude is the 'martyred step'. Hand in hand with the assumption that no one could love a child who is not related to them, comes the common view that anyone who does accept that role must have heroic stature. When there are children from a previous relationship, many couples find that friends and family feel that the adult 'taking on' someone else's children is doing the parent and children an enormous favour. Cherryl was 24 when she met Stan, a 31-year-old widower with three children of three, four and and seven. He had been on his own ever since his wife had died four days after the birth of the youngest child.

We worked in the same office and I thought he was lovely – so kind and caring and he was super with his children. I met them very early on because our firm has a creche and the younger ones were in it, with the seven-year-old there sometimes in the holidays. The eldest was a bit stiff at first but the two youngest were friendly. The real problem we found was everybody seemed to take it for granted I was some form of saint and the reason I was going with Stan was to be a mum to his kids, and they had to get down and kiss my feet or something to thank me! I was with him because I thought he was dynamite and, yes, I'd do the best I could but I wasn't doing anyone any favours, here. It really made things hard because I went through a stage of having to wonder whether Stan loved me or just wanted me as a mother. And that made me quite resentful of them. But I couldn't say anything because everyone wanted to see me as a saint and saints don't grumble or have unkind thoughts, do they?

If you start with the idea that the parent and any children have to be grateful to a new adult simply because they are accepting that part of the package is that 'kids come too', you could set yourself up for a whole raft of problems. Any resentments, angers or split loyalties felt by anyone in the new family become very hard to own up to, to accept or to come to terms with. The fact that these may be understandable reactions to the situation gets lost in the general presumption that everyone is indebted to the new partner for simply being there. Cherryl and Stan started having problems two years after they married but didn't seek help for another four years. By then, their own child was three. Looking at why they had come for help at that time, Stan realised that his new baby was now at the same age his other 'baby of the family' had been when his first wife died. Their problems had come to a head when Cherryl became pregnant and Stan withdrew, becoming silent and unhelpful. He now realised that he had been full of a fear he could not understand, let alone voice, that Cherryl too would die as soon as she had given birth. It meant that when the baby was born, he found it hard to welcome his child or become involved in her care. Cherryl had felt Stan draw away from her but had not understood why and had assumed he no longer loved or wanted her. She was so locked into the habit of not complaining that she felt totally unable to say anything about her own hurt and anger, which grew until it burst out in fights and small complaints. Once Cherryl could stop being a saint, and Stan could face up to his fears, they both were able to sort out their relationship.

There can be added hostility if the new partner triggered a separation or divorce, with many people blaming the new partner for breaking up a 'happy home', even if cracks were visible in the old relationship long before they came on the scene. But this ill will may be just as great if the new partner had nothing to do with the break-up but is younger, more attractive or better off than the previous partner, or simply is seen to be taking too soon the place of someone who has died.

When Asif's first wife died, he turned to Roya, who was a good friend of both of them, for help and support.

She was like a rock to me and my two children and I don't know what I would have done without her. We fell in love and were married a year later. It was right for us but far too soon for her family. My first wife's brother spread a nasty rumour that we had been seeing each other while his sister was still alive and even when I managed to persuade everyone this was a lie, we were still ostracised by her relatives.

Asif soon realised that his brother-in-law had probably been trying to cope with his own grief by whipping up anger against his sister's husband, and this did help him to deal better with the guilt and hurt caused by the unfair accusation.

Why do we find it so hard to have a positive attitude about blended families? One reason, perhaps, is that we all like to believe in the myth of happy families. We all want to preserve the memory of the Golden Age of our childhood, with a *real* family – mum and dad, brother and sister – living together. We tend to assume that this is the best arrangement, the ideal one. Yet many people find happiness, comfort, security and all the best aspects of family life in families where the couple are not married, or where there is a single adult, or where there are two adults of the same sex or where two parents both bring up their children but live apart. The problem is that as a society we are still wary of admitting this. It's as if acknowledging that other, diverse forms of family – single parent families, families made up of gay couples – may be happy too, we may conversely have to accept that what can lie under the surface of an 'ordinary' family may not actually be so perfect after all. Or we may not want to dip into the murky waters of our own childhood, which may not have been as ideal as we'd like to think it was. We might feel superstitious about recognising that different forms of family exist, as if just knowing they do allows disruption to happen.

STEP-FAMILY STRUCTURE

According to the British organisation Stepfamily, there are at least 72 different forms of step-family, depending on whether each adult is single, widowed, divorced or separated, whether you have children living with you or with your ex-partner and whether you have children with the new partner. Becoming a step-child is not an experience confined to childhood either as, increasingly, the parents of adults remarry, after being widowed or divorced late in life! All these people find themselves in blended families, of varying and often advancing complexity.

Rose and Philip have a two-year-old son. Philip has two sons aged 10 and six by his first wife and a 14-year-old daughter by a girlfriend he lived with for four years. He never sees the girl but has regular contact with his oldest boy. His ex-wife has remarried and she and her new husband have a young daughter. This man has a child by a previous relationship, whom he never sees.

Geoff separated from his wife Anna two years ago and they have divided their large house into two apartments. She lives on the ground floor, he is at the top and their three children have rooms in the middle with free access to both living areas, seeing both parents daily. Geoff and Anna live totally separate social lives, coming together for events that involve their children such as Parent/Teacher nights at their schools.

Adele is 12 and her parents divorced when she was seven. Her father lives 200 miles away from her mother and she only sees him one weekend a month and for a week each in the summer, winter and spring school holidays. Adele's mother has a partner, who is single, and who recently started living with them. Her father has a new wife, also previously single, who is now pregnant.

Ray is 27 and has lived with his partner Nick for three years. Nick is 35 and has a daughter and a son by his ex-wife Sue. In spite of some opposition from her parents, Sue was sympathetic and supportive when Nick came out and encourages both him and Ray to see the children as often as possible. Ray is referred to as an uncle but between the three of them, Sue calls him a step-father and has given permission for him to request a Parental Responsibility order.

Keith and Pauline are getting married soon. She has two daughters, who stay with their father on weekends and for half the school holidays. Keith has a son who lives with his mother and sees him every other weekend. Pauline's daughters are very hostile to the boy so Keith collects him from his mother's and takes him out, never bringing him to the home of his new family. Keith's ex-wife has a long-term boyfriend who has his own apartment. Although he lives with her and her son during the week, he keeps his own place because otherwise his wife (from whom he is separated) would not let him see his three young children.

Sally and Bill broke up last year when she found he had been unfaithful, for the fourth time in two years. Their 10-year-old daughter lives with Sally and sees her father, who now lives with a girlfriend (not the one involved in the break-up). Visits were once a week at first but Sally refuses to speak to Bill so arrangements often go wrong, particularly when Sally decides at the last moment to change them or Bill is late. Sally feels she has no one to turn to, particularly since her father is dead and her mother remarried six months ago. Sally's mother now has two step-children, whom Sally cannot bear to see or even talk about so she seldom contacts her mother in case they or their own children are there too.

James's parents divorced when he was seven. He was sent to boarding school while his five-year-old sister stayed with his mother. He spent alternate holidays with his father and his new wife and his mother and her new husband. When he was nine, his mother and her new husband had a child, and a year later another. When he was 12, James's mother died and his step-father remarried a woman who had her own children. She was happy to take on her new husband's two birth children and his step-daughter but not his step-son, so James no longer saw him. His father, meanwhile, had also had children by his new wife who became increasingly impatient with James. He still visits but everyone seems to assume that, now he is 17, he will soon go to university and fend for himself, no longer having a base in his father's home. A year ago, James's grandfather (his mother's father) also divorced and married a woman with five children and 14 grandchildren. James used to spend a lot of time, particularly at Christmas and New Year, at his grandfather's. Now he, too, has lost contact with James as he spends most of his time with his new wife's family.

Max and Zoe have just got married to each other having both lost their partners two years ago. They had all been friends, and their families had known each other for 40 years. Max has two sons and a daughter, Zoe has two sons and each of them has three grandchildren (at the last count!) All their children and grandchildren came to their wedding and all were delighted and very amused at becoming siblings, particularly since they had grown up together and in many ways had been like brothers and sisters for years. The only 'problem' as they saw it was trying to keep clear in the present and future younger generation's minds who was truly related to whom, simply for the record.

Tony and Kay have one daughter, Heather, who divorced when her son Saul was three. They have always got on well with Saul who saw and stayed with them regularly but lived with his mother, only seeing his father occasionally. When Saul was 10 Heather remarried but it only lasted a year. She then had several relationships before living for two years with the man she eventually married as her third husband. When Saul was 15, Tony and Kay suggested he live with them for a short time, since he was doing badly at school and arguing with his mother and step-father. He is now at university and sees his mother often, but his main home is with his grandparents.

SIGNIFICANT OTHER OR PARENT?

Part of the difficulty with a blended family is that step-parents are usually expected to take on the role of a parent. That is, they are expected to love and care for, discipline and provide for children who are seen as theirs. Which, of course, is where many of the problems start. A new partner may smoothly replace the old one in the adult's eyes, but as far as a child is concerned, a parent is your parent for life. The replacement adult can indeed become a highly significant adult in the child's life, but children will be highly resistant to any suggestion that the real parent be replaced, even if the birth parent has either abandoned or totally abused their position. A child is actually formed by the combination of two people. When you try to remove half of their inheritance by preventing contact with one parent or even by denying that this parent matters to them or ever had a role in their life, you effectively remove or destroy part of the child's very self. It cannot be done, and the attempts to do it or the assumption that that is what the parent's new partner should be doing is what causes the majority of problems within a blended family.

Being a parent is a complex and often contradictory job. You don't just attend to the physical needs of your offspring by providing home and board, you also nurture them emotionally with love and care. But care, as well as being about love and sympathy, is also about trust and acceptance. Parents are there for their children even when the child behaves badly, and even when the child is positively unlovable. And part of the parent/child bargain is that sometimes you can't stand your children or the things they do; sometimes you look at them and feel irritated and bored and want nothing to do with them. You're *allowed* to be negative about your own offspring sometimes because the bottom line is that you do love them and always will. When you're an adult in a blended family, however, negative feelings are the source of enormous guilt. The expectation is that although you must take on the *role* of parent, you can't have the same *feelings*, and that means both the good feelings and the bad ones, too. A step-father or mother is expected to walk in and take on the mantle of the missing parent, perform this function flawlessly and love the child. Otherwise, they may find themselves criticised and they will certainly feel guilty and inadequate. But how can we expect to feel acceptance and love for children we didn't give birth to, if it isn't always there for those we did give birth to? Especially when our society places so much emphasis on 'your own' and insists that it is simply not possible to feel love for another person's child?

In most Western, industrialised societies, we still tend to assume that parenting is a task undertaken by a couple, each of the opposite sex. Traditionally, it takes a man and a woman – and only one of each! – to produce a child, so the assumption is that this is the pattern for bringing one up. Group parenting or parenting by two men or two women makes us extremely uncomfortable. Other societies may not agree and communal living is often very beneficial. (And, of course, don't forget that with new advances in gene slicing and *in vitro* fertilisation, the *man* + *woman* = *child* formula is no longer the only one). But many blended families, who might otherwise have worked out a formula that could operate for them, find the idea that 'only two play' forms a stumbling block. Val and Simon, for instance, separated when their children were nine and 13 and for the first year co-operated and agreed on their care. Simon says:

No divorce is perfect but we were working it out. Nicky and Sally came to stay regularly, and we still went to things like Parents' evenings together, and Val would ring me up and fill me in on what they were doing. We would discuss and make shared decisions about holidays and important matters such as Nick's secondary school and Sal's exam results. It was fine, until I started seeing Pam on a regular basis and the kids got to know her, too. Val suddenly got very uptight. What upset her was Pam being around, even though she never interfered or tried to take over. When Pam and I were married, it all changed. This coincided with Val having a new man of her own and she simply stopped ringing. When I rang she would be evasive, offhand or vague. It was Sally who told me about Parents' nights, not Val and Val made it pretty obvious I was no longer welcome along. Then she and Gerry moved in together. He's a good bloke and he and I get on reasonably well and he is terrific with my children. They're now 13 and 17 and it would make sense to me if we all got together to plan the things that affect us all. I once suggested to Val that we should all go to Nick's school concert together. You'd have thought I suggested having sex in public! She was shocked, outraged, horrified. Her idea is that she and Gerry go to some things, she and I go to others and – reluctantly and only because Nick particularly asked – Pam and I go to some together. But all together – never. It's a pity because the truth is that it's the four of us who are bringing up these kids in a kind of spread-out group marriage and we should all be there for them. Val, I think, simply feels ashamed that we aren't 'normal' and she thinks if we're seen in public together it just

underlines that. I think she also feels it would somehow be indecent
for Pam and Gerald to get to know each other or be seen together,
although of course they have met.

I myself can remember visiting my step-son Alex's primary
school on an open night and walking around with him while his
parents Vic and Jenny spoke to his teacher.

We met the headteacher who immediately assumed since I was an
adult and with Alex that I must be his mother. He breezily
introduced himself and was obviously totally nonplussed when
Alex corrected him by saying, `No, this isn't my mother. It's my
father's partner.' I had assumed that it was common knowledge
that his parents lived apart – he never seemed to keep it a secret.
In retrospect, perhaps if Alex had called me 'my step-mother' the
man might have taken the situation slightly more in his stride,
but at that stage Alex fiercely resisted any suggestion of mother
status because he had one perfectly good mother of his own and
didn't need another. As it was, the poor man totally lost the thread
and was speechless, to Alex's delight! But it certainly underlined to
me the fact that the rather fragile compact we had arrived at
for our 'family' was viewed strangely, to say the least, by other
people.

＿＿MOTTOES FOR A SECOND FAMILY＿＿

Even though step-relationships are now common, we still persist
in seeing them as abnormal, odd and somehow shameful. There
are three truths that anyone in a blended family should have
framed on their walls:

> You are not alone. Blended families are just as normal as
> any other type of family, and just as natural.

No family, blended or otherwise, is perfect. Being a 'good enough' parent is the best you or your partner can realistically hope for in *any* circumstances.

The problems you face are likely to be the result of the situation rather than because you are uniquely inadequate or the children are uniquely wicked.

Appendix 1
SECOND FAMILIES AND THE LAW

General beliefs about blended families are not conveyed solely in the expectations and assumptions of friends or family. The step-relationship has little standing in law. A step-parent has no automatic parental rights. This would seem understandable in a case, for instance, where a couple were living together without formalising their relationship with marriage. You might expect the partner to have no status in law, even if a child is living with the couple. And you would equally see the difficulty in formalising the status between children and the new partner of one of their parents if the children remained with the other parent. However, British law at present goes even further. No legal relationship exists between a child and their parent's new partner even in a remarriage where the children are permanently resident.

You could say that this state of affairs underlines, quite properly, the importance of the continuing ties between children and their birth parents. A legal and binding connection between a child and one parent's new partner weakens the link between the child and their other birth parent. The need for sustaining such ties has already been discussed in chapter 8. But the origin of such a law does not lie in an understanding of, or care for, the child's needs. On the contrary, it's an expression of our society's views on parenthood. Animals might reject another creature's offspring out of instinctive need to preserve their own genes and not advance anyone else's. In a sense we do the same by, in law, only allowing for the acknowledgement of our own issue and not accepting someone else's child to be taken for ours.

FACT POINT

In the UK, since April 1993, child maintenance has been the responsibility of a Government agency called the Child Support Agency. Under the 1991 Child Support Act, this agency can require parents who do not live with their children to pay an amount of money as a contribution to their care.

The parent with whom children live full-time is called the parent with care. The parent who lives apart is called the absent parent. Even if the child spends time with both parents and they have equal responsibility, the one the child spends fewer nights with is the absent parent.

A formula is used to work out each parent's income and their essential expenses and then to assess how much should be paid.

Some members of a re-formed family may consider this an advantage. An adult living with their partner's children has no immediate or automatic legal or financial obligations towards a child who is not theirs. The new Child Support Act, which came into force in April 1993, does not apply to step-parents and indeed states 'New partners of either parent will not be expected to pay anything towards the child support maintenance of children who are not their own'. Marrying someone who has children gives you absolutely no responsibilities for those children. Of course, this works both ways because it also means you have absolutely no rights over them either. This does not only apply to large decisions, such as their schooling or where they live. It also applies to day-to-day decisions such as what they wear, who they befriend and whether or not they get their ears (or anything else!) pierced. But the fact is that if a child lives with you, they will be eating your food and sharing your home which means you will be looking after them in many ways. The conflicts that arise from taking on emotional and financial responsibilities for children while having no rights over them comes up again and again in the difficulties experienced by all members of restructured families. And there is another catch. If a child has been eating your food and sharing your living quarters, you *assume* a responsibility for them as time passes. If the relationship with their parent breaks up, they may still be able to lay a claim on you for the maintenance you have given to continue. And if you die, they may also be able to pursue a claim against your estate. So you do acquire responsibilities for them in time. The problem is that the legal grey area may not help anyone in this situation to resolve the ambiguities and the resentments that could have come about, or been increased, by the legal presumption of non-accountability.

Many adults in this situation would happily assume these responsibilities. You may feel that you and they form a family, and indeed as far as the census takers are concerned you do, even though in the eyes of the law there are no binding ties. Up until the Children Act of 1989 children whose parents were divorcing or separating were considered to be the property of their parents. Custody of the children, care and control and access to them may well have been fought over in the courts with the parents' views of what was right and necessary being uppermost. The Children Act has changed the emphasis so that what is most important now is not what the parents want but what is right for the children. We no longer accept parents' rights to fight over ownership or access to children, but are trying to enforce each child's right to have access to both parents. For this reason, in the place of concepts such as custody and access – which see the situation from the parents' point of view – we have new terms: **Parental Responsibility, Residence Orders** and **Contact Orders**. We also have a new presumption when it comes to making decisions about the best course for children in separating families and new ones, which is 'Only meddle if the situation really isn't working' (also known as, 'If it ain't broke, don't fix it!').

A child's parents both have Parental Responsibility if they were married at the time the child was conceived or born, or if they later made the child legitimate by marrying, even if they are now separated or divorced. The only situation in which parental responsibility can be taken away from you is if your child is adopted, at which point he or she is no longer yours to care for. An unmarried father does not have automatic parental responsibility but he can apply to the courts and get it, although he may under certain circumstances have it removed from him. Other people, such as step-parents or grandparents, can be granted parental responsibility. Giving step-parents or grandparents parental responsibility does not take it away from the birth parents. Birth parents, married or not, can apply for a residence or a contact order. So can step-parents, guardians and anyone who has shared a home with the child for at least three of the previous five years. Anyone who has the support and consent of the people who currently have parental responsibility can also apply.

Courts can make a Residence Order, stating where and with whom a child should live. This can be made out to more than one person, so allowing children to divide their time more or less equally between parents and other significant adults. The Court would only make an order, however, if it can be shown that the child would benefit more from an order being made than allowing the people concerned to work matters out for themselves. It's worth noting that just having a child living with you does not give you parental responsibility unless you already have it. Having a residence order made does give the adults named parental responsibility.

Unlike an Access Order, which implies that one parent is gaining admission to something belonging to the other parent, Contact Orders emphasise that it is the child who has the right to have contact equally with both mother and father. A contact order requires the parent or guardian the child lives with to let him or her see the other parent, or whoever is named in the order. It can also specify that children can have contact by phone or letter. Unfortunately, although a contact order requires the adult with whom the child lives full-time to let him or her see the other adult, it can't make the other adult comply if they choose not to. As with residence orders, the courts will usually only make such an order if it can be shown that the child will benefit from one being made.

The court can also make a **Prohibited Steps Order** and a **Specific Issue Order**. These set out particular actions that one parent wants to prevent the other from doing, such as taking a child abroad or to see a person or types of events when they are together. Or it gives directions about a specific issue, such as the type of education one parent feels is important or inadvisable.

Step-parents can put their relationship with the children on a legal footing by adopting them. Adoption makes children your own, to all intents and purposes. You then have full responsibilities for them and full parental rights over them, even if the birth parent married to you dies. The only difference between you and a natural parent is that you didn't give birth to the child. Adoption by step-parents is unusual, however, and will only be granted if there are exceptional circumstances and no better way of giving the child the stability needed. Another way is by applying for a Residence Order. A residence order says they should live with you and puts you *in loco parentis* – in the place of a parent. While the children are in your care you act like a parent and have responsibilities for and some rights over them.

However, having parental responsibility still does not mean the law acknowledges them as your children, and this can cause all sorts of problems in particular circumstances. When it comes to making provision for the people you care about and care for, don't assume anything – either that the right people will inherit your goods and money after your death or that the right people will take on the task of looking after your children – unless there is a properly drawn up will or a document appointing them. If you die without a will – intestate – your *own* children will inherit, but not until they reach the age of 18. In a blended family, this could put your heirs in a very difficult financial situation, as Sonia and Tania found out to their cost.

Ivan's wife died when their daughter, Tania, was five. Two years later he met Sonia and after a year they started living together. When Tania was 11 Ivan was killed in a car accident. Ivan had not left a will so all his property went to his daughter, but since she was not yet 18 it went into trust until then. Sonia and Ivan had, out of habit, kept separate bank accounts and each been responsible for paying different bills, with Ivan's name alone on the mortgage. Under the circumstances, Sonia could not manage repayments on her own and the house had to be sold with the money going into an account held for Tania when she became 18. Sonia had to struggle to keep the two of them and the result was that she became bitter and depressed, angry at Ivan, and herself, for leaving her with the situation. By the time Tania had reached the age of 18, the two of them were on terrible terms and Tania left home on her birthday, with a large sum of money but no longer speaking to her step-mother.

Don't assume the people you care about and care for
will inherit after your death
or that the right people will look after your children
unless you make proper legal provision.

Neither pre-nuptial nor cohabitation contracts are binding under British law. And since British law follows marriage and blood lines, a step-child can usually only inherit from a step-parent if they are named in a will or have been adopted by the step-parent.

If you, or any member of your family such as your own parents, want a step-child to inherit, you will have to specify this correctly in a will. John, for instance, left a will but he had not been clear enough when drawing it up to have the result he had intended.

Paula was a divorcee with three children, aged 11, 13 and 14, when she fell in love with and married John. He brought them up as his own and they all got on well with him until, after six years of marriage, Paula and John had a child of their own. When their second baby was born two years later, Paula's three became distant. The two eldest had already left home to go to college and the younger one left home early, as soon as she had finished school. Relations were frosty for the next 20 years, with them only visiting at Christmas, if at all. When John died, he left a substantial amount to Paula but the bulk of his estate was left 'to my children'. There was no doubt in Paula's mind that, in spite of their disagreements, John had intended this to refer to all five children. But because they had always borne the brunt of the elder children's hostility, John's and Paula's two children insisted the money was for them alone and because John's step-children were not specified in the will, the courts could only agree with them.

In law, you get what is *said*, not what is *meant*. This is why it is so important to ask for and follow legal advice over the details of blended families. Even though you feel there is a clear family connection, the law may not see it that way. This not only applies to taking a child into your family, it also applies to having one made part of someone else's. When a child is adopted, their legal connection to former relatives is severed, even if they continue to be in contact and everyone involved still considers them part of the family. Donald's family had not realised this which led to him losing out.

Donald's father died when he was two and his mother remarried. Her new husband loved the boy and when their own child was conceived, suggested he adopt Donald so he would be as much his own son as the new baby. When Donald was 19, his grandfather – his birth father's father – died, leaving a substantial amount of money in his will 'to my grandchildren'. Since Donald had been adopted and he had not named each grandchild individually he was not considered in law to be one of them and received nothing. If his grandfather had changed his will after the adoption and explicitly said Donald was still to be included, he would have been.

A step-parent can obtain a Residence Order either by applying through the courts with the agreement of both natural parents,

FACT POINT

A common occurrence is for a child to bear their father's surname after a separation while living with their mother, and for the mother to then change her name. She may go back to using her birth or a former name or she may take on the name of a new partner. What about the child's surname? Legally speaking, you would need to ask the Court for permission for a change. Unless they have been adopted, children can only have the surname of their birth parent taken away from them with the consent of both birth parents. If the father wanted the child to keep alive a connection with him, he can refuse permission. Even if he has no opinion on the subject, the courts will want the child to retain that link until old enough to make a mature decision for him or herself. It is worth noting, however, that there is no law in this country that forbids anyone to use any name they please, as long as there is no intention of doing so to commit a crime.

or after having lived with the child for three years. A Residence Order gives parental responsibility until a stepchild is 16 years old, or it can be extended to 18 years. You are only likely to obtain an order if it seems better for there to be one rather than no order at all. In both residence orders and adoption, the first consideration is the best interests of the child, which is as it should be. What is best for the child, however, is not always what is best for the parents. The uncertainty and anxiety felt by parents and step-parents who feel their position to be insecure may in itself cause difficulties for everyone concerned.

When Alan and Joanna set up home together, he had two daughters aged seven and 10 from his previous marriage and she had a son aged six from hers. Alan and her boy got on well together. Alan's daughters would stay with them two to three nights every week and he had a shared residence order for them with his ex-wife. Joanna had the same for her son with her ex-husband but Alan had no formal responsibility for the boy. When they had been living together for a year, they asked the court to make a residence order in favour of Alan but Joanna's ex-husband objected, feeling this would weaken his links with his son. Since the boy seemed to be well adjusted and it was Alan who felt left out, this was refused.

The importance of making a will cannot be overemphasised. This may not only forestall the painful results of an unexpected death but also help to establish a framework for the relationship of child and new adult. Deirdre made a point of making her step-son Paul her next of kin and feels this move was part of a new, stronger relationship between them.

Paul is the least materialistic person I know but when we moved to our new house, when he was about 21, I made a point of having a fresh will drawn up. This makes him the designated next of kin to

*both myself and James after each other. The money is nothing to
him, but when I told him what I'd done, he was touched and
pleased. I was saying, in no uncertain terms, that he is the next
most special person to me after his father and I meant it.*

Parents may also need to agree their attitudes to details such as
consent to medical treatment, foreign travel and obtaining a
passport, kinds of education and religious affiliation. The non-
residential parent still has a lot of say in their child's life but this
needs to be used to keep concerned involvement, not to complicate
matters or compromise the child's well-being. Strictly speaking,
unless you have made explicit arrangements, a parent's new
partner is not *in loco parentis* even if they are caring for the child
full-time. This could mean that they would be unable to give
consent for medical treatment if it were asked and the birth
parent was not available, which could be inconvenient in some
circumstances and downright dangerous in others.

You may need to consider and discuss the arrangements for
legal responsibility and residence of the children involved.
Consider whether the arrangement you settle on has been agreed
between you – a so-called gentlemen's agreement – or whether
you feel it necessary to go to court for a Residence Order or even
to apply for adoption. While you may feel that adoption would be
the best way of achieving stability, don't forget that the courts are
highly unlikely to allow it unless there is no other way of acting
in the child's best interests. Asking for the help of a counsellor or
conciliator may be a very necessary move, both to understand
and accept the legalities involved and to hear and take on board
the views of everyone concerned.

All the adults involved also need to decide what they want to
happen in the event of a tragedy – the death of one or both of the
birth parents. If one parent dies, will the assumption be that the
child will automatically live with the other? If the child has lived
full-time with one parent and their partner, will they stay in that
home in the event of that birth parent dying? The views of even

very young children should be taken into account when you are considering these very difficult and painful decisions, and you would be advised to ask for the help of a counsellor or a conciliator in getting it sorted out. It's a very human failing to avoid talking about tragedy, in the superstitious hope that if you don't mention it it won't happen, and if you do talk about, it will. If you leave such important decisions to fate and they then have to be settled by law, you might find that the rigid, official rulings may not be in the best interests of everyone involved. Remember that, in law, the step-parent in the partnership has no rights over the children whatsoever unless these have been negotiated and officially agreed. There are many pitfalls that can be avoided if you make the proper provisions for them. It would be worthwhile re-reading the section on law and making sure that you have not left your family or yourself vulnerable should the worst happen.

Appendix 2

USEFUL ADDRESSES

Most of the following addresses are of the organisations' main offices. Check your local phone book first, and if there is no entry contact the head office for the address of the nearest local help that is available. Many of the organisations, particularly if they are small and voluntary, do change addresses frequently so you may need to contact a similar organisation or Directory Enquiries to find out current details of where they are.

STEPFAMILY: National
   Stepfamily Association
Chapel House
18 Hatton Place
London EC1 8RU
Tel: 0171 209 2460
Helpline: 0171 209 2464

Child Support Agency
PO Box 55
Brierley Hill
West Midlands DY5 1YL
Tel: 01345 133 133

British Association For Counselling
1 Regent Place
Rugby
Warwickshire CV21 2PJ
Tel: 01788 578328

Relate
Herbert Gray College
Little Church Street
Rugby CV21 3AP
Tel: 01788 573 241

London Marriage Guidance
   Council
76a New Cavendish Street
London W1M 7LB
Tel: 0171 580 1087

Marriage Care
Clitherow House
1 Blythe Mews
Blythe Road
London W14 0NW
Tel: 0171 371 1341

Cruse Bereavement Care
Cruse House
126 Sheen Road
Richmond
Surrey TW9 1UR
Tel: 0181 940 4818
Bereavement line: 0181 332
7227

Child Guidance Clinics
see under Child and Family
Guidance in your local phone
book

Institute of Family Therapy
43 New Cavendish Street
London W1M 7RG
Tel: 0171 935 2946

Citizen's Advice Bureau
see your local phone book

Divorce Mediation and
    Counselling Service
38 Ebury Street
London SW1 0LU
Tel: 0171 730 2422

National Council for the
    Divorced and Separated
13 High Street
Little Shelford
Cambridgeshire CB2 5ES
Tel: 0116 270 0595

Gingerbread
16-17 Clerkenwell Close
London EC1R 0AA
Tel: 0171 336 8183

One-Parent Families
255 Kentish Town Road
London NW5 2LX
Tel: 0171 267 1361

National Family Mediation
9 Tavistock Place
London WC1H 9SN
Tel: 0171 383 5993

Solicitors' Family Law
    Association
PO Box 302
Orpington
Kent BR6 8QX
Tel: 01689 850227

Legal Aid Board
85 Gray's Inn Road
London WC1X 8AA
Tel: 0171 813 1000

PARENTLINE
Endway House
Endway
Hadleigh
Essex SS7 2AN
Tel: 01702 554782
Helpline: 01702 559900

Parent Network
44-46 Caversham Road
London NW5 2DS
Tel: 0171 485 8535

Rights of Women
52-54 Featherstone Street
London EC1Y 8RT
Tel : 0171 251 6577

Women's Aid Federation
PO 391
Bristol BS99 7WS
Tel: 0117 963 3542

INDEX